Undaunted is filled with compelling stories and life-changing revelation. It will challenge you to let the light and hope of Christ shine through you into the dark places of this world.

— JOYCE MEYER
Bible teacher and bestselling author

Christine's devotion and loyalty are immeasurable. Her own story of redemption frames the core of her belief system and fuels her endless passion. We are confident that *Undaunted* will unlock freedom not only in the reader but also in the individual worlds we influence, resulting in multitudes being blessed.

— BRIAN AND BOBBIE HOUSTON
senior pastors, Hillsong Church

This book will be like an alarm clock going off in the depths of your soul. The thread of God's lavish grace and captivating mercy extended to us — and then through us — is woven throughout every chapter. Chris has given us what the church has been waiting for, dying for: a reminder of God's love and then a kick in the pants to get busy living differently!

— PRISCILLA SHIRER
Bible teacher and *New York Times* bestselling author

I love Christine's undaunted heart. And I love this page-turning message. These words will rattle lose the cords of fear and uncertainty that hold us back from fulfilling our own calling. Then with carefully studied truth, Christine ignites a fresh passion deep within the soul of her reader. Don't let fear make you miss out on the best in your life. Read this book today!

— LYSA TERKEURST
New York Times bestselling author,
Women of Faith speaker,
and president of Proverbs 31 Ministries

If anyone can motivate you to chase after God's calling in your life, it is Christine Caine. *Undaunted* will stir you, challenge you, and dare you to take a giant leap into the adventure of a sold-out life for Christ.

— CRAIG GROESCHEL
senior pastor of LifeChurch.tv,
author of *Soul Detox: Clean Living
in a Contaminated World*

Christine does an amazing job of using stories from her own life to help teach you that you are called and able to experience a life of boldness, courage, and purpose. I am thankful for Christine's example and leadership to encourage us all to be *Undaunted.* This book is long overdue from one of the world's greatest voices in the body of Christ.

— JENTEZEN FRANKLIN,
senior pastor, Free Chapel;
author of *New York Times* bestseller *Fasting*

Christine Caine dares to shine a light into the dark, grimy places of life-altering circumstances: human trafficking, loss, grief, identity, and abuse. A woman of undaunted courage, she confronts the challenges with godly perspective and practical application points, valuable for any reader dealing with the call to tackle adversity and to affect true change.

— DR. ED YOUNG
senior pastor, Second Baptist Church
Houston, Texas

UNDAUNTED

CHRISTINE CAINE

UNDAUNTED

Daring to do what God calls you to do

 ZONDERVAN®

ZONDERVAN

Undaunted
Copyright © 2012 by Christine Caine

This title is also available as a Zondervan ebook. Visit www.zondervan.com/ebooks.

This title is also available in a Zondervan audio edition. Visit www.zondervan.fm.

Requests for information should be addressed to:

Zondervan, *Grand Rapids, Michigan 49530*

Library of Congress Cataloging-in-Publication Data

Caine, Christine.
    Undaunted : daring to do what God calls you to do / Christine Caine.
      p. cm.
    Includes bibliographical references.
    ISBN 978-0-310-33387-6 (Softcover)
    1. Self-actualization (Psychology) — Religious aspects — Christianity. 2. Power (Christian theol-
ogy) 3. Human trafficking — Prevention. 4. Church work with prostitutes. 5. Prostitutes — Religious
life. I. Title.
BV4598.2.C355 2012
248.4 — dc23   2012016762

All Scripture quotations, unless otherwise indicated, are taken from The Holy Bible, *New International Version®, NIV®.* Copyright © 1973, 1978, 1984, 2011 by Biblica, Inc.™ Used by permission. All
rights reserved worldwide.

Scripture quotations marked MSG are taken from *The Message.* Copyright © 1993, 1994, 1995,
1996, 2000, 2001, 2002. Used by permission of NavPress Publishing Group.

Scripture quotations marked NKJV are taken from the New King James Version. Copyright © 1982
by Thomas Nelson, Inc. Used by permission. All rights reserved.

Scripture quotations marked NLT are taken from the *Holy Bible, New Living Translation,* copyright
© 1996, 2004. Used by permission of Tyndale House Publishers, Inc., Wheaton, Illinois. All rights
reserved.

Any Internet addresses (websites, blogs, etc.) and telephone numbers in this book are offered as
a resource. They are not intended in any way to be or imply an endorsement by Zondervan, nor
does Zondervan vouch for the content of these sites and numbers for the life of this book.

Published in association with the literary agency of David O. Middlebrook, 4501 Merlot Avenue,
Grapevine, Texas 76051.

Cover design: Grey Matter Group
Cover photography: Veer® / Corbis® / © Daniel H. Bailey
Interior design: Sarah Johnson

Printed in the United States of America

To my husband, Nick,
and precious daughters, Catherine and Sophia.
You are God's greatest gifts to me.
I am forever grateful.

For we are God's handiwork, created in Christ Jesus to do good works, which God prepared in advance for us to do.

EPHESIANS 2:10

Contents

Foreword

I've wondered what it would be like to visit with the apostle Paul — the globe-trotting, gospel-proclaiming, chain-breaking trumpeter of grace.

I've imagined a good chat with Mary, the mother of Jesus — the simple village girl who, upon learning that she would be virgin *and* pregnant, told God: "Whatever you say, I'll do."

I've envisioned a conversation with Esther — the liberator from nowhere. Out of the shadows she stepped, and because she did, a nation was spared.

Paul. Mary. Esther. Turns out, I've met all three in the person of Christine Caine.

She has the spunk of a Paul. She's scarcely on the stage, or at the dinner table, before you hear her passions: Jesus, her family, and the forgotten girls of the slave trade. You know where she stands. And you know whom she loves. It's contagious, this heart of hers. Wonderfully infectious.

She has the obedience of a Mary. Who would have pegged a Greek-born, Australia-raised, blonde pistol as a world-changer?

Yet, just like the mother of Jesus, she brings Christ to the nations. Everywhere Christine goes, from South Africa to Eastern Europe, she radiates hope.

Especially to the girls to whom she is an Esther—the millions of teenage girls who find themselves in the throes of Satan's cruelest concoction, the sex trade. These young women should be becoming exactly that, young women. They should be listening to music, reading books, and flirting with guys. Instead, they are locked into brothels, beaten, raped, and treated like livestock.

Their only hope? Jesus Christ. And Jesus has chosen to work through people like Christine. Christ appears, not just in her name, but in her face, resolve, grit, and joy. She makes the rest of us want to love the Jesus she loves in the manner she loves him.

I pray you will read this book. If and when you do, you'll discover what I have: God has given our generation a Paul, Mary, and Esther. And her name is Christine Caine.

God has given our generation the opportunity to make a difference in the vilest atrocity of the century.

After reading this book, I resolve to do more.

I hope you will too.

Max Lucado

chapter 1

The *Schindler's List* Moment

The Greece I found that Wednesday afternoon in March 2010 was not the one I remembered from my honeymoon fourteen years earlier. There were no stunning, whitewashed buildings. No lapis-blue tile rooftops. No festive music. No outdoor market with vendors selling freshly pressed olive oil, mouth-watering feta cheese, fresh cantaloupe.

None of that. This afternoon the streets were empty, black, wet. The normally crystal-blue Mediterranean pounded dark and rough against the Thessaloniki shipping port. Strange how fear, not just the season—this long, hard winter—changed everything.

Is this how they see it? I wondered.

"They" were fourteen young women, mostly Eastern European, recently rescued from sex trafficking. But they hadn't begun their journey as women—they'd been mere schoolgirls when lured from homes in the Ukraine, Bulgaria, Georgia, Albania, Romania, Russia, Uzbekistan, and Nigeria. Sixteen year olds. Seventeen. Eighteen. Girls who should have been giggling about music and basketball games, worrying about what to wear to school—not how to survive the next minute.

Securely hidden in a safe house run by The A21 Campaign, the rescue ministry my husband, Nick, and I had launched just six months before, we were to speak face-to-face this dreary afternoon about a part of Greece I'd never known. I kept reminding myself: *This is not a movie. This is not "reality TV." This is real. This is real.*

The young women and I sat together in awkward silence. How does one speak of unspeakable depths of shame and agony?

Nadia braved the waters. Haltingly, she told how she had been raised in a village in Georgia at a time of war and deprivation. Her family possessed an abundance of love but not food. Poverty consumed them. For years Nadia lived on dreams: dreams of escaping the hunger, dreams of a world away from the ravaged village, dreams of becoming a nurse. If she were a nurse, like the ones she saw dress the wounds of soldiers in her village, she could get away. She would travel. She would see a beautiful world, a world in which she had a helpful role to play.

But girls in poor Georgian villages did not go to school beyond the second grade. They needed to learn only how to cook and clean, not to read and write. What man, after all, would want to marry a woman more educated than he? Wasn't that all that was expected—to marry, keep house, provide children, depend on one's husband for everything else?

Nadia, an obedient daughter who desperately wanted to please her parents, tried to push aside her secret dream. Yet embers remained in her heart.

So just three weeks before her seventeenth birthday, when a man approached her group of friends at their bus stop and told of opportunities to work in Greece, those embers began to glow brighter. The man told the girls that Greece was beautiful and that people prospered there. He said there were many good-paying jobs for waitresses, hairdressers, shop assistants. He said there were jobs just waiting for nurses.

The man gave her a brochure and said a meeting the following Friday evening would provide all the details.

For the next week, Nadia felt blinded by the light of opportunity. Her dream seemed so possible, so close. On Friday, she arrived early at the village community hall and found a seat in the front row. Several dozen other girls trickled in after her. The room was filled with excitement, chatter. Some men introduced themselves as agents and gave a compelling presentation of the opportunities in Greece. They promised a bright future. They passed out the necessary paperwork for obtaining passports and work visas and patiently helped the girls fill out the forms.

Nadia left the community hall full of hope. She ran home to tell her parents that she had the chance to start a new life. She could not only get education and training as a nurse and live a life of helping others, but she could soon send home money for her entire family.

Her parents were concerned. Greece was so far away. But the embers of hope burned in them too. Perhaps their daughter would be able to get ahead as they never had. Perhaps she could find a profession, earn a good income. She could be their key to new lives too. After much discussion, they reluctantly agreed to let her go. They drained all their accounts, selling what they could, even borrowing, to scrape together the fee Nadia would have to pay the hiring agents for her passage to Greece. Her dream—happiness, success, prosperity—became their own.

Nadia was met at the airport in Greece by a woman from the hiring agency who spoke no Russian. Nadia spoke no Greek. But despite that confusion, she went with the woman to an apartment building, where she was shown a room that she supposed would be hers. The woman left, and Nadia began to unpack.

Within minutes, her nightmare began. Several men rushed in and locked the door behind them. They beat and raped Nadia repeatedly. She tried to fight back. She screamed for help until she no longer had a voice. But for every protest, every scream, she received more abuse, more torture.

Confused, scared, ashamed, in pain, and broken, Nadia retreated to a dark place deep inside.

For two weeks, the beatings and rapes continued.

Finally, Nadia was told about her job. It wasn't in a hospital. It wasn't in a restaurant. It was in a brothel. Her new life was to be a sex slave. "If you do not do as we tell you, we will kill your family," she was told.

Surely, she concluded, people this evil would make good on those threats. Besides, they had taken all her papers, including her passport, and she did not speak Greek, nor did she have any idea where she was. Even if she escaped, she knew she wouldn't get far, let alone make it all the way back home to Georgia. Nadia felt utterly alone, though the men she had believed were hiring agents surrounded her twenty-four hours a day, seven days a week. When they weren't in her room, they stood guard just outside her door and sent in a constant flow of customers with whom she was forced to perform unmentionable acts — up to forty times a day.

No longer sure there was a God in heaven — why would he have allowed this to happen? — Nadia pled with him anyway. *Let me die,* she prayed. *Oblivion would be better than this.* The silence, the horror, pulled her deeper into despair. No ember of her dream remained, let alone any hope of returning to a life with her family, to things familiar and free.

One day when the guard left her room, he forgot to lock the window. Though her room was on the third floor of the apartment building, Nadia scrambled onto the balcony. *Maybe, if I am lucky, the impact will kill me. Oh God,* she prayed, *let the nightmare end.*

She jumped.

A woman passing by saw a girl throw herself from a third-story balcony and crash onto the pavement below. Horrified, she ran to Nadia, who, miraculously, was uninjured.

Nadia heard the woman speak—and was amazed that she understood that the woman was asking if she was all right. Had she died? Was she in heaven? No. Another miracle. This woman was real! And she spoke Russian! She wanted to help! Quickly, Nadia told her of her plight.

The woman gathered Nadia from the pavement and took her to the police station, where they filed a report. Then the police hid Nadia in a safe house to protect her from the traffickers.

✦

One by one that March afternoon, the girls around me shared stories like Nadia's. Most had been raised in impoverished, ex-communist Eastern European nations. Each had come to Greece expecting legitimate employment. All had brought with them dreams, hopes, and aspirations to do something more with their lives than their own families had ever dreamed possible. All of those tender, youthful dreams had been shattered beyond anyone's worst fears.

What shook me most was the realization that, for each of these young women I spoke to that day, there were hundreds of thousands of others still trapped in the sex slave trade with no way out—hundreds of thousands of women whose unspeakable pain remained shrouded in secrecy. Silent.

Then Mary from Nigeria told her story. She and fifty-nine other young women had come to Greece in a shipping container.

"Wait," I interrupted. "Do you mean you were contained in a ship?" I thought I'd misunderstood, or that something had been lost in translation.

Mary repeated: She and fifty-nine other young women were brought to Greece in a shipping container.

A container loaded onto a ship? Like the one I'd just had an estimate on from a moving company for shipping my household goods to our new home? "A box?" I pressed. "A container used to carry personal and commercial goods, not people?"

That's right, Mary assured me—a box, a container put onto a ship. When she and the fifty-nine other girls arrived at the port the day of their departure, they thought they were traveling to good-paying jobs in a land of opportunity. Instead, they were greeted by hiring agents who said there were complications with the paperwork. Either travel by container, the girls were told, or lose your deposits and any future opportunity to work abroad. Either make the voyage in a shipping container or turn around and go home.

"Our families had given everything they owned to pay for our passage," Mary said.

So one by one, bewildered and frightened, the girls entered the container. When the last girl was inside, the door was slammed shut and they heard a lock snap into place. They sat frozen in darkness.

"Then the bubble broke! The bubble broke!" Mary exclaimed.

"What bubble?"

The filter, she explained, that allowed oxygen to circulate in the container. It stopped working, and the inside of the cramped box suddenly became not only lightless but airless as well.

I gasped, imagining the oxygen being rapidly depleted, the heat building, the women gulping for air in complete darkness.

The journey in the sealed container was gruesome. Half the girls died from lack of oxygen. The other half, the stronger ones, were near death themselves. They had nowhere to sit but in their own vomit and feces, since they were forced to relieve themselves on the container's floor.

When the men at port opened the container, Mary said, they recoiled, appalled by the smell of death, decay, excrement.

One of the dead was Anna, Mary's best friend. Anna had died an excruciating death, suffocating as if buried alive. But Anna was real, Mary insisted to me that day. Anna had existed. And Anna must be remembered.

The hiring agents preferred to forget. More interested in quickly getting what they referred to as their "shipped goods" from the dockyard, they hustled the living to small apartments nearby, where, like Nadia, the girls were repeatedly raped and beaten.

Before sunrise one morning (Mary had lost all sense of the passage of time), the girls were loaded into small rubber boats and taken across the Mediterranean Sea to a Greek island. This was the first time they realized that the original voyage had not even taken them to Greece. They had been brutalized in Turkey. None of the agents' promises had been kept.

In the boat, Mary felt a surge of hope: The Greek Coast Guard was doing a routine check that morning—unusual for that hour, Mary later learned. She hoped that, unlike the crew on the docks, the Coast Guard could not be bribed to turn a blind eye. Mary's captors showed signs of panic. Though she was freezing, sleep- and food-deprived, broken, and in shock, Mary's hope grew. Rescue! Justice! Once caught, the traffickers would face a lengthy imprisonment.

And for that reason, these men would do anything to avoid being caught.

They began throwing the girls overboard.

Only five of the approximately thirty girls—those who had been strong enough to survive the deadly voyage in the shipping container—escaped drowning that day.

Those five were hidden among their captors when the Coast Guard came aboard. When they finally arrived in Athens, the girls were taken to a brothel, where the nightmare of the Turkish apartment was repeated. Daily, Mary and the others were forced to participate in unspeakable encounters with dozens of men. Mary sank deeper into despair, wishing that she, too, had suffocated in the airlessness of the container or drowned in the Mediterranean Sea.

The horror continued for weeks. Or maybe it was months— Mary couldn't tell. But one day, anti-trafficking authorities, responding to a tip, raided the brothel. Mary and other girls were herded into the back of what appeared to be a police van. Were they being rescued? If hiring agents could be evil, couldn't police be as well? Uncertain and broken, Mary and a dozen other girls were raced to another apartment building. Police rushed them inside, where the girls waited in fear and resignation. But instead of beatings and rape, they were given rest, food and water, peace.

Though no longer in a physical prison, Mary remained silent, constantly tormented by recurring nightmares. The daily horror may have ceased, but the pain screamed nonstop.

Mary was safe but not yet free.

+~+

Stunned, I sat quietly for a moment after Mary finished her story. Around me, the young women at the table remained quiet too, almost reverent. Yet inside me, a storm of thought surfaced. Questions hammered at my broken heart: *How could this possibly happen in our world today? No matter how much money is involved, how can anyone be so depraved as to make sex slaves of others—let alone make it an international operation, enslaving not just one girl but hundreds of thousands, again and again and again?*

Sonia, a Russian girl who had arrived at the shelter the previous day, interrupted my flood of thought. "Why are you here?" she demanded, her eyes narrowed with suspicion. "Why did you come?"

Her tone was angry, and I felt the distrust behind her question: Was I who I said I was? Was I someone who could help? Or was I, like the hiring agents, untrue, unfeeling, evil?

How can I make her understand, I wondered, *that I, too, know what it is to be trapped, enslaved, with seemingly no way out, no way forward, no way back? How can I make her see that, as bleak as her enslavement has been, there are prisons just as black inside oneself, prisons into which Sonia and many of the girls sitting here may have retreated? How can I make each of these girls know that I care in the same way someone once cared enough to come to me in my pain?*

Oh God, I prayed. *Help me help them!* I breathed deep and looked at Sonia for a long moment.

"There is only one rescuer I know," I told Sonia and the rest of the women, "with the power to free us from the darkest prison. That rescuer is the God I love, who loves us so much he left everything to come for us, to free us. He is the one who made us, each of us, for a unique purpose and a magnificent destiny. He makes right what the world makes wrong. His plans are for good, not for evil. His ways are straight and merciful. He came to give me a hope and a future—and to give you one too. His promises are true. His love is full of forgiveness and peace, joy and kindness, grace. He is the true rescuer. He saves us from any prison, whether physical or emotional or spiritual, the ones we're forced into and the ones we fall into on our own. He chooses us. He can make all things new. He loves us without condition, unrelentingly, forever. He loves us broken, and he loves making us whole again. And he asks those of us who love him to love others the same way. To choose them. To be agents of his hope, his forgiveness, his grace. He asks us to join him in rescuing others.

"That's why I'm here," I said. "That's why I've come."

Sonia's eyes filled with tears. I could see her grappling with the concept of unconditional love, the meaning of grace, of all things being made new. All the *whys* and *hows* of what I'd said furrowed her brow. All the *what ifs* and possibilities had died in her long ago. Yet here I was, resurrecting them. *What if there are good agents and true promises and a merciful God who loves me and chooses me and can lift me from the impoverishment, the betrayal and fear, the hurt and horror? What if . . .*

No! Sonia could not believe all this. It was too good to be true. She knew all about promises too good to be true. The risk of allowing hope to reenter her life, only to see that hope dashed again, was too much. Her anguish turned back to anger, and she pushed back from the table. "If what you are telling me is true," she yelled, "if what you say about your God is true—then where were you? Where have you been? Why didn't you come sooner?"

Why didn't you come sooner?

The girls around me didn't move. No one spoke. But I could feel their eyes on me, their minds screaming that same question. I felt like Mary in that container, the weight of such a heartfelt cry pressing in on me like suffocating, airless darkness. I could barely breathe.

Why didn't you come sooner?

The question seemed to echo. In the emotional power of the moment, the image of Sonia across the table, with her angry, anguished eyes, shimmered and morphed into that scared nineteen-year-old girl trapped in a room for one year, forced to service at least twenty-five men every day. That image morphed into another: a girl confused, hurt, and alone, engaging in self-mutilation or substance abuse or binge eating as a way of dulling her emotional pain. And then another, poor and starving, unable to feed or protect her family. And then another image: of children this time, suffering and dying from malnutrition. More images: depression, suicide, abuse . . .[1]

The faces became as grains of sand, so many. One hundred? Two thousand? A million? Too many. So many grains of sand that they melded together, indistinguishable, flowing like waters of the sea, an ocean of faces floating there for a minute, bobbing in and out of focus, hazy, distorted in the depth of suffering, loneliness, need, despondency, hopelessness. An ocean of faces going under, going down. I heard their sinking cry. I heard myself cry out as well, going under in a black despair.

Why hadn't I come sooner?

On the surface, of course, there was a reasonable answer. So reasonable—an unassailable excuse: I hadn't come because I didn't know about their plight. How could I have come before

I knew? How could anyone blame me for not fixing a problem I didn't know existed?

But I didn't offer that excuse. I didn't offer it because the depth of their pain, the reality of their suffering at the hands of cruel and evil men, deserved more than excuses. And I didn't offer it because I was suddenly thrown into a memory that put not only the suffering and plight of these women, but my reaction to it, in startling perspective.

A scene from the movie *Schindler's List* began to roll through my mind. The movie, produced and directed by Steven Spielberg in 1993, is the story of Oskar Schindler, a Gentile businessman in Nazi Germany who saved the lives of more than a thousand Jews by breaking the law to keep them working in his factories. In a powerful scene at the end of that movie, Schindler, played by Liam Neeson, is being thanked for what he has done by a crowd of those he has rescued—just before he flees for his own life. The grateful Jews present him with a ring on the inside of which is inscribed a saying from the Talmud: "Whoever saves one life saves the world entire." But, distressed, Schindler says, "I could have got more out. I could have got more. I don't know ... if I had just ... I threw away so much money. You have no idea ... I didn't do enough." He looks at his car. "Why did I keep the car? Ten people right there." He pulls a pin from his lapel. "This pin. This is gold. Two more people ... and I didn't. I didn't." And then he collapses into tears, overcome by the realization not of all that he *did* do, but that the pin in his lapel was apparently worth more to him than the lives of two people.

This moment, sitting at that table in Thessaloniki with those women so recently saved from slavery and yet still so devastated, was my *Schindler's List* moment. It was my moment of wondering what, in my life, had been my golden pin like Schindler's, the thing so precious to me that it never occurred to me to use it to ransom the life of someone else.

Whoever saves one life saves the world entire.

I would not offer excuses.

"I don't know," I stammered at last. "I don't know why I didn't come sooner." Such weak, small, light words for such a weighty question. "I am sorry. I am so sorry. Please forgive me."

The silence became even more pronounced. Time seemed to have stopped. Nothing else mattered to me at that moment but these girls, their despair—and what healing God could bring to them. Though the silence seemed to last for an eternity, I felt so clearly present, so tuned into the now.

"I want you to know," I said with new conviction, "that I have now heard your cries. I have seen you. I see you now." I turned to Mary. "I *see* you, Mary. And when I see you, I see Anna." I turned to Sonia. "I see you, Sonia." I looked intently at each girl seated at the table. "I see each of you. I hear you. I know you by name. I have come for each of you."

I wanted to see these girls as Jesus saw them—not as a sea of needs, but as individuals he had called by name and chosen one by one and loved. I heard his words before I spoke my own: *Tell them I have their names written in my book.*[2] *That I came to give the good news to the poor. To heal the brokenhearted. To set the captives free. Tell them these promises are for here. Now. As well as for eternity.*[3]

"You will no longer be hidden," I told Sonia. "From now on, wherever I go, I will tell people you exist." I focused on each girl, one at a time. "I will ask them the very same question you've asked me. I will not sit back waiting, hoping, wishing, for someone else to do something. I promise you: I will *be* the someone. Now that I have found you, I will find other girls like you. I will do everything I can to stop this."

✦

Long after leaving that meeting, Sonia's question rang in my ears, shook my mind, unsettled my heart.

Why didn't you come sooner?

I offered them no excuses that day, but I did know that

there were reasons. Reasons that, when we hear God's call, when we feel that gentle (or not so gentle) urging of God's Spirit for us to make a bold step, take a risk, serve others, save a life, commit—we so often hold back.

It's because we don't feel empowered.

We don't feel qualified.

We think we lack the courage, the strength, the wisdom, the money, the experience, the education, the organization, the backing.

We feel like Moses when, from out of the burning bush, God called him to speak for him before Pharaoh. And Moses answered, "Pardon your servant, Lord. I have never been eloquent. . . . I am slow of speech and tongue. . . . Please send someone else" (Exodus 4:10–13).

Not me, God. I'm afraid. Weak. Poor. Stupid.

Unqualified.

Daunted.

Not long ago, that is exactly how I would have responded.

But it has never been my desire to be *daunted*, to be afraid, to be unable to respond to God's call. Is it yours? I doubt it. I think that you, like me, want to be able to say instead, "Here am I, Lord—send me." We don't want to sound like Moses, stammering around in search of excuses.

And we don't need to. Because, just as God gave Moses exactly what he needed to accomplish great things for God, he will equip us in just the same way. If he calls us to slay giants, he will make us into giant slayers.

God doesn't call the qualified. He qualifies the called.

And that is what this book is about. It is about what I call the "normal Christian life"—living boldly and courageously in the face of great difficulty, and amazing the world by beating the odds, for God's glory. It is what the apostle Paul meant when he told Timothy, "The Spirit God gave us does not make us timid, but gives us power, love and self-discipline" (2 Timothy 1:7).

There is no shortage of ways life tries to daunt us, to render us incapable of following the bold and valiant plan God has for us. This book is about how to move past that—how to become *undaunted.*

And as I traveled away from that meeting that day, I thought of my own story. If anyone ever had a reason to feel unqualified, to feel *daunted,* it was me. And the reasons for that went back to things that happened before I was even born . . .

part 1

GOD KNOWS MY
NAME

chapter 2

I'm Not Who I Thought I Was

I had just closed my mouth around that first, long-awaited fork-ful of beef vindaloo—extra spicy—when my cell phone rang. I looked down, ignoring the midday chaos of the office dining area. Kathy. My sister-in-law. I savored the steaming vindaloo and considered letting her leave a message on voicemail. No. She rarely called in the middle of the day.

You'll just have to wait, I told my impatient stomach. I set down my fork and pressed the answer button on the phone.

The moment I heard Kathy's voice, I knew something was wrong: "Christine, George needs you. Can you talk to him? He's very upset. He just received a letter from the Social Services Department that claims that he's not your biological sibling. He was adopted at birth by your parents."

What! I couldn't believe what I was hearing. "Let me talk with him," I said.

George came on the line, sounding distraught. He read the letter to me. "What do you make of this?" he asked.

"It's got to be a mistake. Social Services obviously sent this to the wrong person. Call the supervisors at Social Services immediately and tell them about this. Tell them it has to be a mistake. Then call me back to let me know how it went."

I hung up and pushed away my plate of food. The beef vindaloo that had seemed so delicious a few minutes before now didn't interest me at all.

How could someone have been so careless? Didn't they realize that a mistake like this could turn someone's world upside down? Why hadn't they taken more care in addressing the envelope, or in noticing which envelope they stuffed the letter into?

My phone rang again, interrupting the storm rattling inside me. "George!"

He was breathless. "Christine, it's true. They have an entire file on me. They told me that my birth mother has been trying to contact me, and they gave me the name of my biological mother and father. They told me where I was born. I have an appointment to go in and see the Social Services people tomorrow. They said they will tell me everything."

"It *can't* be true, George!" My racing heart beat over the sound of his mounting confusion. "This is just a big mistake, a mess. We'll get it straightened out." Though I tried to sound confident, I felt my own confusion rising with his.

An entire file ...

"I have to talk to Mum about this," George said. "I can't wait—I'm going over there now." I agreed, and told him I would meet him there.

I grabbed my purse and raced to the parking lot, my mind spinning in circles. *It's impossible—of course George is my brother. We grew up together. It's a ridiculous mistake. But ... what if it is true? After all, there's an entire file—no! It can't be true. What's George going to say to Mum?*

I was so shaken that for a full five minutes I couldn't remember where I'd left my vehicle. I eventually found it—right where I had parked it—jumped in, and drove to Mum's house in record time. For the second time that afternoon, I braced myself for what I was about to encounter.

WAS EVERYTHING ABOUT TO CHANGE?

As I walked up the path to the front door, I thought about all of the memories my family had created together in this home: The endless afternoon soccer games with friends in our front yard, the gathering place for all the kids in the neighborhood. The birthday cakes and homework dug into at the kitchen table. The Christmases around the tree. *How could all of that not have been just what it seemed to us then—a normal family living life together? And yet what if this letter George received was true? Was everything about to change?*

Oh God, I prayed, *give me wisdom, guidance, grace, and patience.* I stepped through the doorway. What I saw stopped me in my tracks. George, his wife Kathy just behind him, was handing Mum the letter from Social Services.

Mum's hands shook as she scanned it.

There was fear, not confusion, in her eyes. And I knew. *It's true*, I thought. *It's true. My brother is adopted.* Time seemed to stop. I couldn't breathe. I felt pinned in place, only able to watch as tears streamed down Mum's face.

She looked at my brother. "I am so sorry you found out like this, George. We never meant to hurt you. We love you. I couldn't have loved you more if I had given birth to you myself. We loved you before we even laid eyes on you—and once we did, at the hospital, we never considered you anyone else's but ours. A closed adoption was the only option we were given, at your birth mother's insistence, and we were advised to never tell you that you were anything else but our very own. I never imagined that your birth mother would try to contact you, or be allowed to. She signed a form giving you to us totally. I don't understand! The adoption laws must have changed." Mum looked down at the letter, slowly shaking her head in disbelief. She sobbed, repeating, "I couldn't have loved you more, I couldn't have loved you more." Then, "We didn't want you to even think you were unwanted or rejected. We never dreamed you could find out, especially after all of these years. One of the last things I promised your father before he died was that I would never tell you."

I felt paralyzed. The scene playing before me seemed surreal, more like a movie than my own life. *How could this secret have been kept from my brother for thirty-five years? How could Mum and Dad never have told us that George was adopted? Why had I never had the slightest suspicion that George and I were not biological siblings?*

And yet . . .

This explained the mystery of why George is six-foot-four and I am five-foot-three. And why I have perfectly straight, light hair while he has curly dark hair. I almost laughed. *How could I have overlooked such glaring dissimilarities all these years?* A sudden thought sobered me: *What other family secrets did I not know?*

The question overwhelmed me. The tension, fears, and tears were rising, so I decided to do what any good Greek girl would do in the eye of a storm.

I headed straight to the kitchen to prepare something for everyone to eat.

Raised according to the philosophy that food is the answer to most things, I functioned on autopilot to make extra-strong Greek coffee and rummage in the pantry for some baklava. Our heritage had taught me that when in doubt about what to do or say, turn to cooking and eating, and a solution will present itself. So I set everything on the table, hoping the combination of caffeine and sugar would recalibrate us. Then I took a deep breath and called to George, Kathy, and Mum.

We gathered around the same table where our family had shared meals and ordinary moments and milestones for more than twenty years. Only now the atmosphere around this table wasn't the same. Our trust had been breached. There was a schism where before there had been none. We sat on the edge of it, so shaken we didn't know where or how things were going to settle, or whether more things would crumble and fall. Uncertainty rumbled in the air and in the very pit of my stomach. With one letter, with a single seismic conversation, everything I'd thought I knew about our family had been turned upside down, inside out.

HINTS AND SECRETS

For an awkward moment we all sipped our coffee. Then Mum cried as she told us that after several years of trying unsuccessfully to conceive, she and Dad had been given an opportunity to adopt. They had decided to take it, while continuing to try to have children naturally. It had been a time of great anticipation, she said, repeating, "We loved you before you were born. We loved you before we laid eyes on you."

I realized that, amazingly, neighbors and extended family members must have known—yet said nothing about it to us kids. *How can you keep such a thing secret? You can't exactly hide one day not being pregnant and the next coming home with a baby! How was it possible that so many people knew about this for decades, yet over the years never let a hint slip?*

And yet . . .

And yet there *had* been hints, though they had been unclear to me at the time. I remembered an incident around this same kitchen table when I was eleven years old. Mum had been peeling onions, preparing our dinner, as George and I and our younger brother, Andrew, played the board game Trouble. Somehow our conversation turned to adoption. I'm not sure how that happened, but I remember telling Mum that even if I were adopted I wouldn't care, because I loved her and Dad so.

"I can't even imagine anyone else being my parents," I said.

My brothers each echoed my comments. *I can't even imagine anyone else being my parents.* I drew in a long breath. And for all these years, I had thought it was the onions that made Mum cry that day.

Dad called on the phone a few minutes later, as we siblings continued our board game, and Mum immediately told him that we had been talking about adoption. She left the room as she talked, and her voice dropped to a whisper. *What is it I'm not supposed to know?* I wondered at the time. *What is it they don't want me to hear?*

I strained, unsuccessfully, to eavesdrop, but heard nothing. Impatient, my brothers whined that it was my turn to play, and I turned back to our game as Mum returned to the kitchen. She busied herself with the pans as she prepared dinner. And that was that. From that moment until this, the word *adoption* was never again mentioned in our home.

Now, as George sat with his head in his hands, struggling to make sense of the new reality, I said to Mum, "That day …" I wanted to know now what was kept from me back then. "Remember that day," I repeated.

Mum nodded. "I remember every detail." She told us how she'd come undone by the very mention of the word she and Dad had worked so hard to keep us from hearing, from understanding. When Dad called, she was ready to burst with anxiety.

"Shouldn't we tell them?" she'd pressed.

She and Dad had reasoned together. The truth might hurt us. Maybe it was best to keep things as they were, they agreed, and never speak of it again.

Now here it was, that secret truth, being talked about at the kitchen table. But, with the confession over, Mum's face relaxed. Her tension eased. She seemed relieved, freed by the truth now in the open.

And yet for the other three of us, tension remained. Kathy was motionless. George sat speechless.

He's in shock, I thought.

The silence, the stillness, took on an energy of its own. To break the strain, I reached for another piece of baklava.

"Christine?" Mum asked. "Since we're telling the truth, would you like to know the whole truth?"

I dropped the baklava.

My heart skipped a beat, possibly five. The way she had asked that question could mean only one thing. I searched her eyes, hoping for some sign that I was wrong. Finally, I choked out, "I was adopted too."

How much more bizarre could this day become?

What do you do when you have been living all your life, more than three decades, with facts that you *thought* were true, only to discover that so many of them weren't facts at all?

What else in my life was a lie? What other secrets were there about our family, about the life I'd thought I knew so well? Could I trust anyone or anything else? I felt like I was living in my own version of the movie *The Truman Show*.

Remember that film? How Truman discovered that his home, workplace, and world were not real at all, but rather constructed as part of a television studio that contained hidden cameras everywhere? Truman began to suspect, and then proved, that his friends and associates, from best friend to mailman to man on the street, were merely actors, each hired to play a fictional role in his pretend, if unscripted, life. Everyone around him knew that his life was merely *The Truman Show*, the most popular television series in the world. Everyone knew, that is, except Truman. I thought about how he discovered the lie, the hidden cameras, the actors who were simply doing a job, and how it rocked everything he believed about who he was and what his life consisted of. The revelation shook his sense of self to the core, as if his world had just tumbled into the sea, leaving him adrift in confusion. I thought of his sense of sadness, anger, fear, deception, betrayal.

I understood exactly.

For several long moments, Mum, George, Kathy, and I tried processing this rattling loop of emotion. The fact that I didn't say anything was in itself a miracle to anyone who knew me. I could feel my family's eyes fixed on me for some reaction.

Finally, I managed a single question, one that for me was of the utmost importance. "Am I still Greek?"

George, Kathy, and Mum burst out laughing. I couldn't help but join them. We so needed that laughter to de-intensify the moment. It had been such a hard, long afternoon, full of one shocking revelation after another. With its first burst, the laughter relieved the tension. And it did something more. It ushered back some of our familiar trust, our unquestioned love for one another ... and with that, one more revelation.

THE THINGS I KNEW FOR SURE

As it began to sink in that so much of what I'd thought to be true about my life was a lie, a surprising thing happened. Instead of being completely shattered, an assurance rose within me.

True, I had just discovered that I wasn't who I thought I was. I had no idea who my biological parents were; I knew nothing about them. I didn't know if I had been conceived out of love, a careless one-night stand, an affair, or a rape. When my birth mother gave me up for adoption, was she reluctant about it? Had she felt forced? Or was she eager to be rid of the inconvenience? I didn't know if she and my birth father had stayed together. Did he even know that I existed? Were they still alive? Why had she never contacted me? Did I have other brothers and sisters somewhere?

There was so much I didn't know. I was amazed that so many questions can flood your mind in a split second, from one moment to the next.

And yet ...

Despite all that, there was also so much I knew for sure. So much that nothing my mum had said, nothing she could possibly say, would turn into a lie.

Nothing Separates Us from God's Love

Without thinking about what I was doing, I stood, looked at George, then Kathy, then Mum, and said with conviction, "Before I was formed in my mother's womb" — and here I paused to add, unable to resist, "whose ever womb that was — God knew me. He knitted together my innermost parts and fashioned all of my days before there was even one of them. I am fearfully and wonderfully made.[1] Even though I only just found out that I was adopted, God has always known, and he has always loved me. And since *that* has never changed, therefore *nothing* has essentially changed. I may not be who I thought I was, but I still am who he says I am. And I am more. I am loved. I am his."

Mum, George, and Kathy stared at me.

I stared back. They seemed as shocked by my words as by the news about the adoptions. I was a little shocked myself. Even as the underpinnings of my world had shifted radically, they were resettling in a more secure place. Even as things seemed to be falling apart, the truth of God's love was holding me together. And that truth was: I knew he loved me, unquestionably, unconditionally, whether I was adopted or not. The truth was: His love is relentless, unyielding, passionate, unfailing, perfect. A feeling of peace, supernatural peace, engulfed me. I was okay. Everything was going to be okay. That may seem like an odd conclusion, in light of the fact that my life, or at least everything I'd thought I knew about my life, was unraveling before my eyes. Nevertheless, I felt undaunted by it all, because of an unchanging, never-failing truth, a truth I clung to tenaciously: God was in control of my life.

Of course, I thought, *nothing like a few quakes to test that belief. But did I really believe God is who he says he is?*

Yes. I did. God's promises were real: I love you. Nothing can separate you from my love. Nothing can take you from me.[2]

37

Mum and George and Kathy must have wondered, *In the face of all that has been unleashed this afternoon, how can you possibly feel such peace and positivity and resolve?*

It may have seemed a miracle—but it wasn't a mystery ...

The Truth Sets Us Free

For more than a decade, I'd immersed myself daily in God's Word. I had memorized countless verses about God's love for me. I desperately needed his love, and when I read how he loved me, how he had a place for me, I soaked it up.[3] I meditated upon those words, pondered and prayed over them. I found life in them. The words contained promises that excited me so much that I began to preach them. I told myself and others about the unconditional love of God, how each one of us is created by him and for him and for a purpose.[4] I shared how God never leaves us nor forsakes us, that he is always with us in every circumstance, that his right hand upholds us, that he is our very present help in time of need.[5]

Now those promises were holding me. What Jesus promised was real: When you believe God is who he says he is, when you hang onto him and his Word in faith, his truth sets you free.[6] The truth you store up in silence comes back to you in the storm, and it lifts you away as on a life raft from the fears and disappointments that would otherwise pull you under. When you abide in his Word, he abides in you.

Despite the day's unsettling revelations, I could feel the unconditional love of my heavenly Father surround and engulf me even as I sat there with my family. The truth is, I had been adopted into God's family when I surrendered my life to Christ. Christ was my brother, and God my Father. I needn't be unsettled by the thought of adoption, because I'd already been adopted by God! I was his child. And he loved me, and promised to *always* love me and be right beside me in any situation, even this one.

We Were Loved before We Were Even Born

Mum smiled at me with wonder—and relief. Though I had been shaken by everything that afternoon, I hadn't been shaken *loose*. I wasn't melting down.

My calm gave Mum a glimpse into the power of God's love, and that glimpse gave her courage. She told me about the spring day the hospital called her with the news that I'd been born. Mum had been at the neighbor's, visiting over cups of tea in the backyard. So my grandmother, who had answered the phone, shouted over the neighbor's fence, "We have a girl! We have a girl!"

"I loved you," Mum said. "I loved you before I even met you."

Hearing that from her was like the truth that had brought me to my feet just a moment ago, like hearing an echo of Psalms 139:13–16:

> *For you created my inmost being;*
> > *you knit me together in my mother's womb.*
> *I praise you because I am fearfully and wonderfully made;*
> > *your works are wonderful,*
> > *I know that full well.*
> *My frame was not hidden from you*
> > *when I was made in the secret place,*
> > *when I was woven together in the depths of the earth.*
> *Your eyes saw my unformed body;*
> > *all the days ordained for me were written in your book*
> > *before one of them came to be.*

God knew me and loved me before I was even me. He knew me before I was born, and throughout my adoption, and he knew me even now that *I* wasn't sure who I was anymore. He loved me despite any trouble I found myself in or challenges I faced. I could mess up or melt down and he would love me still. I could be ashamed of where I came from or try to hide who I was, and God would still love me, knowing me better than I knew myself. He loved me when I feared I was less-than. He loved me so much that he would always have my back in any challenge or distress, and he would go before me through anything unknown.

Yes, I thought. *I'm not who I thought I was. I am so much more. I am loved by God, the maker of the universe, the maker of me, and I was loved by him before I was born and will be after I die.*

LOVE WILL CARRY YOU

Mum, George, Kathy, and I were spent. We stood and hugged, but we knew we needed time and space to process everything. We'd withstood as much emotional earthquake as each of us could bear for one day.

I suddenly longed for some normality. Routine. I decided to keep a meeting back at the office.

On the drive back to work, I called our younger brother Andrew (he's biological!) and gave him a quick version of all that had happened. "I'll tell you more later," I said. I was going to have to hurry if I wanted to get to the office in time. Besides, I needed some silence, some think time.

I got off the phone and let myself relax into the familiar motions of driving. I rolled down the windows as I passed favorite buildings and houses, listening to the hum of the tires on the pavement. Familiarity soothed my heart as much as it did my senses. So did God's familiar assurances.

I knew that God cherishes us, because he "so loved the world that he gave his one and only Son, that whoever believes in him shall not perish but have eternal life" (John 3:16). I knew that he claims us, because he said, "You are a chosen people" (1 Peter 2:9). I knew that he carries us because "even to your old age and gray hairs . . . I am he who will sustain you. I have made you and I will carry you . . . I will rescue you" (Isaiah 46:4).

Calmed by those thoughts, I was emotionally tired but strangely at peace. The truth that I'd known all these years seemed real to me in a new way: I'd been adopted by God long before I was adopted by Mum and Dad—and he cherishes me, claims me, carries me.

That is just what love does, I thought. *It cherishes us and claims us and carries us.*

Though Mum didn't carry George or me in her womb, love helped her carry the secrets of our births over all these years because she wanted to protect us.

I walked into the office feeling not heavyheartedness but almost a lightness. The meeting had already started when I sat down. I looked around the room at the faces of my colleagues. Together we were committed to bringing God's love and his promises to kids with eating disorders, kids who harmed themselves, kids who were marginalized and from broken families and in gangs—kids looking for love and a place to belong, to be cherished and claimed and carried.

Though I hadn't planned on it, upon seeing their faces, I decided to share with my team what just happened. "You're not going to believe this," I began.

When I finished telling them about the revelations of the day, the shock I had felt hours earlier now registered on their faces.

"Are you okay?"

"Why didn't your parents ever tell you?"

"And you never had a clue?"

Then, a question I hadn't expected, hadn't yet asked myself: "What are you going to do?"

WHAT ARE YOU GOING TO DO?

Life will eventually turn every person upside down, inside out. No one is immune. Not the mom in the suburbs who finds out her teen daughter is pregnant. Not the husband who is entangled in an affair with a woman not his wife. Not the kid whose parents are strung out on drugs. Not the girl entrenched in human trafficking. Not the boy with HIV or his brother hungry and without any prospect of enough to eat.

Not the woman who finds out her whole sense of identity is based on a family connection that turns out to be a lie.

Not you.

Not me.

But just as life will upend you, so will love.

Love has the power to undo you for fear of losing it, as it did my parents over the thought of George and me discovering our adoption. Love has the power to bewilder, as it does when a baby, new life, comes to you.

God's love, which knows you and claimed you before you were even born, can take you beyond yourself, as it did Jesus, who left heaven to go to the cross and pass through the grave in order to bring us back home. His love can bring you through emotional earthquakes, as it did me the afternoon I was told news that could have flattened me but was carried by God's promises. Love like Christ's can lift you out of betrayal and hurt. It can deliver you from any mess. Love like that can release you from every prison of fear and confusion. And love like God's can fill you up till it spills out of you, and you have to speak about it, share it, spread it around.

"What are you going to do?" my coworkers asked. Well, I had definitely been affected by the news of my adoption. Despite my resolute (or was it desperate?) clinging to God's Word and his promises, I'd have been something other than human if I hadn't been emotionally stunned by what I'd learned that day. But I was not going to allow myself to be daunted by it. I had watched so many people allow life-changing news like this drive them into anger, resentment, and depression, to push them to question their identity and self-worth and value. I knew how potentially daunting this news could be if I did not choose, on that day and for all days ahead, to bring each of my thoughts and feelings into compliance with what I knew of God. I chose to trust that, in ways I could not yet see, God would use this. God would not only uphold me as I worked through it, but he would honor it by pointing out ways in which this totally unexpected and life-changing revelation could be used for his glory. I had no idea yet what those ways would be. But I had faith that they would come. And as you will see, they did.

What was I going to do? I thought as my meeting with my team turned from my own concerns to those of others, those our group had been called to serve.

Love, I thought. *I am going to love others like I never had before.*

chapter 3

Number 2508 of 1966

I was home alone preparing a meal when the doorbell rang. My fingers dripped with lemon juice from the bowl into which I had just placed chicken pieces to marinate for the night's barbecue. I ran for the door, wiping my hands on a towel as I went.

A deliveryman smiled. "Mrs. Christine Caine?"

"That would be me."

"I have a registered envelope here for you. I just need your signature."

"Sure," I said absentmindedly, still thinking of all I had to do in the kitchen. "Where do I sign?"

He pointed to a line where I scribbled my name, staining his receipt book with a smear of lemon juice. I smiled apologetically and took the envelope inside.

It had been quite a while since I had signed for anything, even at the office where most of our business correspondence went these days. *Who is sending registered mail to my home address?* I scanned the envelope, which looked official, with my name and address typed front and center. "Department of Community

Services," the imprint in the upper left corner read. My heart skipped a beat.

It's here. Just weeks ago, after a full year of wrestling with whether to do this, I'd written to the Department of Community Services to ask for all the information I could get about my adoption. The decision had been torture. Did I want to know more about my biological parents? Did God want me to know? How would it make Mum feel? I didn't want to hurt her, but below the surface, all those questions simmered, a natural curiosity. Who were my biological mother and father? Where were they now? Did I look like them?

I had decided to take it one step at a time. I would write to get the information. After that, I could decide whether to pursue things further.

Now I might be holding the answers to all my questions in my hands. I fingered the edges of the envelope, thinking how thin it seemed for something of such monumental importance. For a few moments my fingers twitched a little, torn between ripping the envelope open and waiting. *No,* I decided finally, smoothing a finger along the seal. *Not just yet.* I walked back to the kitchen, gently placing the mail on the dining table as I passed.

At least a dozen times that afternoon I found myself staring across the room at it. *Why not just go open it? Why am I so hesitant to read what's inside? What am I so afraid of, anyway?* The questions looped over and again until, finally, I realized my issue. Even though I knew God loved me passionately, I had no idea what my biological mother and father thought of me. If they thought of me at all. *Why did they put me up for adoption? Do I really want to know? What if I don't like the answer?*

"This is ridiculous," I said, staring at the potatoes. I put down my knife and walked into the dining room, wiping my hands on my jeans. *Here goes.* I took a deep breath and ripped open the seal.

The first piece of paper on the slim stack inside was headed, "Particulars of Child Prior to Adoption." I reread the title.

"Particulars of Child Prior to Adoption." Then I reread it again. And again. And once more.

Scanning the first page, I saw my biological mother's first name for the first time.

Panagiota.

I stared at it, my eyes held there, unable to move beyond it. *Panagiota. Pah-nah-YAW-tah.* I reread it and pronounced it in my head over and over again. *Panagiota.* One of the most common first names for a Greek woman, derived from the name of the Virgin Mary, a name that means holy, complete. *So I am Greek, after all,* I thought. The name wasn't foreign to me, having been raised in a Greek household. And yet ...

WHAT'S IN A NAME?

Reading that name shocked me as much as hearing for the first time that I was adopted.

I had known that there was a woman out there who'd given birth to me. But to see her full name, a name other than Mum's, whose name I had printed on every legal document for my entire life, more than thirty years — it stopped me cold, with a power I hadn't expected. Suddenly, in my heart, not just my head, Panagiota was real. She was more than a name in a tiny box on this legal document, more than the shadowy, ghostly, faceless figure of "birth mother" that I'd carried over this past year. She was a whole person, a real life with an entire history that was part, a hidden part, of my own story.

I wondered what she looked like. *Did I resemble her? Was she young when she had me? Older? Did she like moussaka or fish and chips? Greek music or English? Movies? And what kind — comedies? Thrillers? At the store as a girl, did she wander as I had from the aisles of dolls into the book section? After school, did she make her way to the soccer fields for a game with the guys instead of practicing ballet with the girls?* I thought of all the things that had set me apart from my family growing up, things that had seemed a mystery to them. But those things might have been Panagiota's style, her way—simply *her*.

Now that I knew her name, this search was no longer just about me. I could no longer think only of myself. Now I thought of her as well—Panagiota. *What questions do you have of me? What has your life been like? What happened to you? Do you ever think of me? Did you ever tell anyone that I exist?*

For a long while I sat, stunned by the difference a name makes. Panagiota had at one time been just a girl, her life ahead of her, with no idea she would one day give birth to a daughter she would give away. And though she did give me up, we were still part of one another, and there was so much more I wanted to know beyond what her first name could tell me.

I read on.

Below the box with her name was another box, this one marked "Father's Name." I took a deep breath. Inside that box was one word.

UNKNOWN

Unknown? I lingered over this word, trying to understand how someone so important to me could be reduced to simply this. Somewhere, somehow, more than thirty years ago, Unknown came together with Panagiota to conceive a child, and the only record of his involvement with her, with me, was this. Seven letters, one word, and that single word seemed so inadequate.

I know more about my dentist, who I see once a year, than I will ever know about the man who is my biological father.

Then my eyes moved to the next line. Something sucked all air from the room. Time froze. I felt stomach-punched. Was I seeing correctly? Was I reading this right? Next to a box marked "Child's Name" was another single word; printed in big, bold, black strokes, another seven letters.

UNNAMED

ONE OF THE NAMELESS

It's said that the punch that knocks you out is the one that you never saw coming. I never even imagined this particular of my birth.

I'd had many conversations over the past year with my close friends about my adoption and the circumstances surrounding my birth. Did my biological parents know each other? Did they love each other? Was I an accident in the heat of one night's passion? Maybe they weren't equipped to handle a baby and thought it best for me to go to a couple with resources or means, more know-how or experience. Maybe they felt forced by their situation. I even prepared myself to accept the possibility that my biological mother and father, if he were even still in the picture, just didn't want me.

Yet in all my conversations, never once had I questioned who I was at my core, my very essence. My identity was in Christ. I knew that. *Whatever they think of me*, I'd resolved, *God loves me.*

But now one word, just seven letters long, mocked me. *Unnamed? I was unnamed until adopted? No one even cared enough to give me a name?*

I could no longer hold back the tears burning at my eyes. They streamed down my face as invisible words between the lines on the document said: *You weren't important enough to name.*

Worse, beneath that word *Unnamed*, something else reinforced my shock: a number.

I wasn't just *Unnamed*. I was Number 2508 of 1966.

What? I felt like I was having an out-of-body experience. I saw myself, holding that paper, the official record of my entry to planet Earth, and on that paper I was described like something off a production line. Like an airline flight, a car model, a ZIP code, a digit on a calculator, a safety deposit box, or any of a myriad of other inanimate objects or sequences. That nameless, faceless number could represent anything. Yet here, right on this piece of paper, number 2508 represented me. I was nothing more than a number.

But everything in me screamed otherwise. I wanted to shout: *I have a name! I am a person! I am Christine, a human being, created in the image of God himself and filled with his purpose.*[1] *I am the girl who once hoped to play table tennis for Australia in the Olympic Games, the woman who relishes chick flicks while eating popcorn with salt and butter, who loves reading, who craves dark chocolate-covered licorice.* How could number 2508 reflect that I was a real living, breathing person with likes and passions, aversions and fears, hopes and dreams?

I sat immobile a long time, staring through a blur of tears at the official records of my birth:

UNNAMED

NUMBER 2508 OF 1966

Air, I thought suddenly. *I need air — and caffeine.*

I went to the kitchen to brew an extra-strong cup of coffee, and all my questions came with me: *How could you carry a child for nine months, feel the heartbeat and the twists and turns inside you, then go through labor, and not have some name for this little being, this new life, this part of you, to whom you gave birth?* I couldn't imagine a single possible answer.

I looked at the clock and was shocked back to reality. Dinner!

I finished cutting up the last of the vegetables, put them in a dish and into the oven, and set the timer. I poured my coffee, looked heavenward, and prayed, "God, help me handle this." I grabbed my Bible and the adoption papers and headed to the couch in the living room. If I was going to face any more sky-falling facts, I'd do it with his Word in hand . . . and with prayer.

I pulled the next piece of paper from the stack — an extract from Panagiota's hospital records: a partial transcript of her meeting with the social worker two weeks before I was born.

Why only a portion? I wondered. *Why wasn't I sent the entire document?*

I started to read, frustrated not only by the scant information but the clinical, medical tone: "Her estimated date of confinement is the third of October and she plans to give the baby away on adoption. She does not seem to be too emotionally involved with the child. She seems to want to get it all over with and get back to work as soon as possible ..."

Not emotionally involved with the child? Wants to get it all over with and get back to work? The words were like another fist to the pit of my stomach.

Now the room was spinning.

I kept thinking: *This is what I am. Unnamed, from Unknown, and unwanted—and I have the legal documents to prove it.* That idea hurt more than the first shock of learning that I'd been given up for adoption. Having no name, I decided, was just as bad as if I'd been called something horrible: *worthless* or *failed, flawed, defective, deficient.* My mind spun off a dozen other negative labels.

Even though I knew by heart God's promise that I was his handiwork, created for good works,[2] these words struck me like a bunch of sticks and stones:

FROM UNKNOWN

UNNAMED

NUMBER 2508 OF 1966

UNWANTED

Only, strangely enough, I realized, the word *unwanted* appeared nowhere on the record.

I read it aloud: "She wanted to get it over and done with and return to work as soon as possible." *What else could that mean, but "unwanted"?* I scanned the two pages: the "particulars" page, the excerpt of the interview with my biological mother. Together, to me, they shouted *unworthy, incomplete, undesirable, unlovable. Unwanted. Unchosen.*

GOD ALWAYS KNEW MY NAME

Isn't it strange how in doubt and dismay, we do some weird math? We see or hear things and add them up incorrectly. We choose to believe what may be *somewhat* factual but simply isn't true. We accept what someone else has said, forcing us to conclude something false about ourselves.

Why is it always so hard to choose first what God says about us? Why do we listen to the voices of others more than his? If our goal is to be *undaunted*, then we should be especially diligent to not let the lies and foolish thoughts of others daunt us. Labels, insults, attempts to overwhelm and limit and thereby control us — these have no place in the life of the believer. God has freed us, and if we're to live undaunted, we can't allow the maneuvering of others to force us back into bondage.

As I held that paper in my hand and stared at those words, I felt a nudge that I knew came from God: *Open my Word to Isaiah 49*. The voice was as clear and familiar as my own. It was the voice of my heavenly Father: certain, soothing, strong. I smiled for the first time that afternoon.

I may not know who my biological father is, I thought, *but I do know my heavenly Father. I know his voice when I hear it.* And because of that, before I even turned a page of Scripture, I knew this situation was going to be okay. I could hear my Father's voice. He was with me. He had promised to never leave nor forsake me.[3]

I found the book of Isaiah, turned to chapter 49, and began to read at verse 1: "Listen, O coastlands, to Me, and take heed, you peoples from afar!"

Immediately, I knew that God was speaking directly to me. I was sitting in my house in Sydney, Australia, a large island with plenty of coastlands; and being Down Under, I was definitely among a people from afar. *Okay,* I thought. *You have my attention, Father.*

"The LORD has called Me from the womb."[4]

The verse warmed and calmed me. I was not an accident. I was not unwanted. I was not unchosen. God had called me. He had not left me out, had not overlooked me, had not chosen instead someone more gifted, talented, better looking, or smarter. He had called me from the womb before I even arrived on the delivery table.

"From the matrix of My mother He has made mention of My name."[5]

I gasped. As stunned as I'd been when I read the word *Unnamed*, this idea struck me even more deeply. This was the truth: God called me by name while I was still inside my mother. *God named me before this document stamped me as Unnamed. Before I became a number, I had a name. I had always had a name. Yes!*

I laughed. I was chosen before I was even formed in my mother's womb. All the details about who I was and who I would be were determined before I even began to take shape: my eye color and shoe size, the curve of my smile, the length of my legs. God shaped my body and my spirit. He created the sound of my voice and loop of my penmanship, the strength of my grip and capacities of my mind.

I couldn't take my eyes off the phrase: "From the matrix of My mother He made mention of My name."

I felt the Lord speaking directly to me: Your birth certificate may say you're unnamed, but I named you when you still were in your mother's womb. You aren't a number to me. You aren't unnamed. I knew before you were born that you would be adopted and that your adoptive parents would name you Christine. I have chosen you for great things. These documents in front of you don't define you or your destiny. My Word is the final authority on that. And I formed you. Your freedom will be determined by whether you allow what I think and say about you to matter more than what anyone else thinks or says, including your biological mother or workers filling out forms for the Department of Community Services. They have said what you are not. But I say what you are, and you are created in my image, not theirs. You reflect my glory."

I breathed deep and exhaled. God's words were like fresh air, uplifting me as the fog of facts and fiction that afternoon began to burn away.

I lifted my Bible in one hand and with my other scooped up all the papers on my adoption. Both hands held paper that contained words printed in black and white ink. Both contained facts. Yet only one held the truth. I had to choose which of these documents I would entrust with my life.

The choice was so simple.

OUR FAITH MEANS MORE THAN FACTS

You can allow the names you call yourself to define you. You can let the labels that others give you define you.

It's so easy! After all, from the time you're born, and then throughout life, you're put in a box. You're defined by your family of origin, address, education, experience, bank account, credit rating, employer, friends, race, and ethnicity. You're called one thing after another: *poor, spoiled, uneducated, inexperienced, young, old, troublemaker, shy.* You can allow those words and labels to limit you. A teacher, parent, colleague, or ex can call you *loser, fat, ugly,* and *hopeless*—and those labels can stick, can hurt, can damage you because you start to believe them.

Remember that old saying, "Sticks and stones can break my bones, but names can never hurt me"? That thought may help you keep a resilient will, but it's not true about the heart. You can be hurt plenty by labels like *stupid, ignorant, alcoholic, addict, criminal, weak, pitiful.* Names like these can break your spirit as much as physical sticks and stones can whack your body—especially if you believe them and begin to use them on yourself. You can be brought to your knees, stopped in life before you even get started. Even when those names reveal something true about you, they are at best a partial truth—as well as a misleading one. If you allow those labels to loom larger in your heart and mind than the promises of God, they can fool you into missing God's truth about who you are, into not pursuing the purpose God has had in mind for you from the beginning of time.

When there is a fight between your heart and your head, experience has taught me that the best thing to do is pick up your Bible and remind yourself of what God says. Your head can insist that God created you and loves you, but your heart and emotions may keep punching away at that knowledge with thoughts like, *What's wrong with me? I never seem to do anything right!* The blows can give you an overwhelming sense of worthlessness and rejection, because that is what untruth about yourself does. It beats you down and knocks you out.

If, like me, you want to find peace, then you need to do what I did that day. You need to return to the truth of God's Word that will last forever, not meditate on circumstances that will change and fade.[6]

It is this truth that enables us to go into the future undaunted.

GOD CALLS EACH OF US BY NAME

I was not an accident. I am not unknown, unnamed, or unwanted.

Neither are you.

We each arrive on the planet differently. Some babies are loved, prayed over, planned for by conscientious parents. Others are surprises. Some are unwanted by their parents. While some are conceived in love, others are conceived by force. Some babies are born prematurely. Some are born breech. Some arrive by C-section, and others are pushed out in a few minutes. Some are brought home to lovely nurseries, handpicked strollers, handmade cribs. Others get hand-me-downs — or nothing at all.

Some of us may not like or know the circumstances of our birth, but not one of us needs to be defined by or limited to those circumstances. Each of us has the chance to be born again in Christ, a second birth, to connect with our eternal purpose.

Before earth was even created, God says we were designed and made to do good works in Christ — works prepared before the making of the world (Ephesians 2:10). No matter how we got here, no matter the particulars of our birth, we each were chosen in eternity long before we ever arrived in time, on earth. If God created us to do good works of eternal significance, he would not create us ill-prepared for those tasks.

Let these truths settle inside you.

- **God made each one of us.** We may not know what our parents felt for each other or even if they knew each other when we were conceived, but each of us is God's workmanship, not the workmanship of anyone else. We are each a masterpiece, made intricately and lovingly by his own hands. It is *that* that gives us our identity—not simply the identity of our parents.

- **God chooses each one of us.** None of us is an afterthought or an accident. My adoption papers may have identified me only as a number, just another in a series, but God *selected* me individually. He designed me in eternity, designed me to be with him beyond the trappings of time—and he selected you in this way too. You are chosen. This is wonderful news for those of us rejected by society for reasons of race, education, social status, or otherwise. Society has made it clear that it values us not at all—but can that matter when the Creator of the universe has chosen us, individually, by name, for a great mission he would entrust to no one else?

- **God is always with us.** Even if our parents discard us, God never leaves nor forsakes us. Whatever circumstances we encounter, or wherever we may be, God is always there with us, beside us, around us, and within us.

- **He names us.** Before we were given a name by our earthly parents, God already knew us by name.

- **He calls us.** None of us is unwanted. God obviously wanted us because he has called each one of us from the womb. He would not call those he didn't want. God makes each of us specifically for a good purpose to be worked out in time during our sojourn on earth—and he equips us to do those things for which he created us. Just as God has given us a unique identity and a unique name, our purpose may be different than the purpose he gives anyone else—which means that when we find ourselves led by God to champion a cause that other Christians find uninspiring or perhaps even misguided, we shouldn't be surprised. Throughout the Bible, many of God's people felt alone as they set out to fulfill God's call on their lives—because the vision God had given them was uniquely theirs, and was not, at first, understood or accepted by those around them.

- **He saves us.** Like me, you may have been given away by your biological parents, but God has made a way for each of us to be born again. Think of it as a do-over. He wipes away the mess of our past and gives us a brand-new start and a hope for the future—and he promises that to each of us, always.

- **He is our Father.** I may never meet my biological dad—this man listed as *Unknown* on the paperwork I received. I may never know how he looked and what things he liked. You may not know your parents either. But we do know the one who has made himself known to us—our Abba Father (Galatians 4:6). He promises that we can know his voice, and that we will become more like him every day (Ephesians 4:11–24).

No, regardless of what our parents may have planned or intended, from God's perspective there was nothing accidental or unintentional about my birth, or yours.

There are things in our lives, God tells us, that we will not understand (Job 36:26). But he knows. If we're to live successfully, if we're to live undaunted, we must learn to trust that his thoughts are higher than our thoughts, and his ways higher than our ways (Isaiah 55:8–9).

Most of the time, when we humans choose, we choose exclusively—meaning we select something and exclude everything else. A starting line-up is picked for the game, while other players sit on the bench. An intern is chosen for the job, and another candidate will need to wait for her chance to get into the company. An adoptive parent chooses one baby, and others remain at the orphanage.

Yet God chooses everyone, all the time, and he chose each of us first (John 15:16; Ephesians 1:4). He never chooses one person at the exclusion of another. He loves each one of us so much that he paid the price for every person to be forgiven and reconciled in relationship with him.

GOD CHOOSES US ON PURPOSE

God not only chooses us for himself—he also chooses us to do his good works on earth. The amazing thing is that, throughout Scripture and history, it seems that God has chosen the most unlikely and unqualified people to fulfill his plan and purpose on the earth. Most often, the response of those people has been to insist on their own unworthiness. And if they don't—the people around them may do so, loudly and shrilly. And therein lies a danger: If we allow other people to tell us what we *are* and *are not* qualified to do, we will limit what God wants to do with us. We may never get to those who need our help.

I'm so glad I didn't limit God in that way. I'll never forget receiving a letter from the dean of the school of social work at a prestigious university, implying that I was unqualified to work with young people. At the time, I was directing a thriving youth program. To work long-term in youth services, though, the dean said I needed formal training.

Surely he's right, I thought. *I'm technically unqualified to do the very thing I'm doing.* I considered submitting my resignation. Yet something inside me said, *No, don't quit.* And for fourteen years after receiving that letter, I worked full-time with youth, and now I work to rescue young people from the injustice of human trafficking. To the world, I looked unqualified. But God cared more about my willingness than my qualifications.

Even as I tell that story, though, I chuckle as I remember times I've watched, for instance, someone trying to lead the music in a church service and thinking, *I wish someone had told him that, to do this job, he should have some sense of rhythm and be able to sing on key!* There are many roles in God's kingdom for which one must be uniquely gifted, whether in music or art or in relationships. We should be sensitive to the possibility, if we lack those gifts, that God may be leading us in a different direction. But once we *find* that direction, we must not allow ourselves to be deterred.

What is impossible with people is possible with God. We just have to believe that God has called us to go into the world in his name, and not listen to the crippling or even paralyzing labels and limitations imposed on us by others. We cannot allow them to daunt us. Whom God calls, he qualifies—and he chooses everybody to do something specific, something that is part of his design. In fact, the Bible shows us that since the beginning of time, God has chosen the unlikely to do the unimaginable:

- **God called Moses**, who was nearly eighty years old at the time, to tell Pharaoh to let his people go (Exodus 3–4). But Moses, as we discussed back in chapter one, insisted that he was not eloquent and that no one would listen to him. When Moses finally stopped making excuses and did as God told him to, God paved a way for him: through the middle of the Red Sea, across the desert—providing food and water and clothing for forty years—all the way to the entrance of the Promised Land.

- **God called Gideon** "a mighty warrior," and told him to save his people, who were being relentlessly ransacked by their enemies (Judges 6–8). But Gideon, who at the time God called him was working in a hidden place because he feared the enemy, couldn't imagine how God could use a coward to fight for his people. "I'm from the weakest of your tribes," he protested. But God promised: I'll be strong where you are weak. And he was, enabling Gideon, with just three hundred soldiers, to defeat the enemy's army of a million.

- **God called Jeremiah**, a teenager, to deliver news to the Jewish people, but Jeremiah feared that, as young as he was, he wouldn't be taken seriously. God said: "Before you were born I set you apart" (Jeremiah 1:5). So for twenty-four years Jeremiah did all God asked, writing two books filled with God's words. Though the first book was destroyed and Jeremiah was imprisoned, where his feet were put in chains and he was once even thrown into a pit, God sent rescuers and made a way for his message to be delivered.

That's how God works. He chooses each of us to do something for him *despite* our past failures, limitations, and inadequacies. Abraham was old (Genesis 17:1; 24:1), Sarah was impatient (Genesis 16), Noah got drunk (Genesis 9:20–27), Miriam was a gossiper (Numbers 12:1–2), Jacob was a cheater (Genesis 25–27), Jonah ran away (Jonah 1:3), David had an affair (2 Samuel 11–12), Elijah was moody—one minute bold and courageous and the next fearful and on the run (1 Kings 18–19), Peter had a temper (John 18:10), Paul was a persecutor (Acts 8:3; 9:1–2), Martha was a worrier (Luke 10:40–41), Thomas doubted (John 20:24–26), Zacchaeus was short (Luke 19:3), and Lazarus was dead (John 11:14–44). But God had a purpose for each of these people. He chose them. He qualified them. He called them, just as he is calling you and me—to go and do in his name. And when he calls us, the name he calls us by is the one he used in the very beginning (Genesis 1:26–28; 2:20–23): "Good."

I have no doubt that nearly everyone who reads this book has been called by God at some time in the not-too-distant past for a task that took us outside our comfort zone—maybe *way* outside it. We felt like responding as Moses did: "Lord, I'm not eloquent."

"Lord, I'm not good at meeting people."

"Lord, I'm not assertive enough. Send Tim instead—he'll be better suited."

"Lord, I don't really have the education that task requires. The people I'd have to convince would just laugh at me—they all have Ivy League degrees!"

"I'm too old [or young]."

"I'm too out of shape."

"I'm not smart [or hip, or cool, or brave] enough."

Moses and Gideon and Jeremiah would have missed out on their moment in history if they'd been allowed to get by with those excuses. We wouldn't even know their names today. We know who they were because God refused to accept their excuses and insisted they accept his assignment—and then provided them everything they needed to succeed in it.

What's the Mission: Impossible you've been declining because you claim you're not up to it?

And when will you finally accept that appointment with destiny?

WE ARE HIS CALLED AND CHOSEN ONES

The day I learned I was unwanted, unnamed, the daughter of Unknown, could have devastated me. And for a moment it did—until God reminded me that his word means more than anyone else's.

Since that day, I've spoken about it openly and often. I've

shared with others about finding my true identity in Christ. About knowing in my bones that he had chosen me and called me by name. Eventually, I noticed that each time I finished speaking, people would line up and wait long periods to share with me their own adoption stories.

Some women sobbed gut-wrenchingly over children they'd given up for adoption; these women felt overpowering guilt and loss. Others told me how they learned they were adopted, and how afterward they struggled with a deep sense of rejection and lack of identity. Other women shared that they'd chosen abortion—and now felt guilt and shame, sadness and remorse.

I'd not realized that my own story would connect with so many others. But with each conversation, with all the prayers, with every tear shed over all sides of this issue of adoption, I realized that because I knew, despite my past, that I was chosen by God, I could help others discover that they too had been chosen by God and for God, whatever the circumstances of their lives. In other words: Because we know that we're chosen, because we've heard God call our names, we can help others hear God call their names.

Nothing about my birth—or yours—was random or accidental. I was born for this time—and so were you. We were each chosen for a particular, cosmically important task that can be done by no one else. We need to be diligent in listening to God's voice calling us to that task—and in encouraging others to be similarly obedient.

That means no longer overlooking the grocery clerk at the checkout stand or the downcast person we pass on the street. Instead, we should choose to recognize their value, and call out their worth. It means caring enough to help the mom at preschool whose child won't come when called, loving enough to offer a word of cheer or humor to the receptionist at the doctor's office struggling to answer phones and still respond to every question at the counter. It means thanking the garbage man lifting bins at the curb, and recognizing the God-made-

and-paid-for-soul in every person we encounter in a day.

But we won't—we can't—help others know they matter unless we first recognize how much God loves and chooses each of us. And that's a challenge we must face inside.

DO YOU HEAR IT?

Several months after the day I found out I was adopted, I asked my mum about the day she got the call from the hospital that I had been born. How had she felt? What expectations had she had?

Her eyes lit up. With enthusiasm, she explained that she and Dad were desperately hoping for a girl, since they already had a son. But there were no sonograms back then to reveal whether you were having a boy or a girl. Mum was very close to her sister, who had four boys of her own and also hoped for a girl, so they would chat often about names and dreams for me.

One day my aunt suggested, "Why not Christine?"

"I like that," Mum said. And so the decision was made over a cup of tea. There was nothing deep or spiritual in that decision—they just both liked the name *Christine.*

Yet I know that my name, Christine, is derived from the Greek and Latin and means *Christ follower.*

And the Christ I follow has given me another name, too—a name by which he calls me. And he calls you and others by that same name—a simple name; one word; just four letters, like *love*—that rings loudly through time and space because you have been chosen before time, and in his time, and beyond time.

Do you hear it? Can you hear him calling your name? Do you see it, printed there in his book?[7]

He calls us: MINE.

part 2

GOD KNOWS MY
PAIN

chapter 4

Scar Tissue

I opened the door to find Nick on the doorstep with a dozen of the most beautiful roses I'd ever seen. Although we'd been dating for a year and I should have known him well by then, I was still both surprised and impressed. He was truly the most thoughtful, kind, and generous man I had ever known, and seemed to always find a way to make me feel special. And best of all: Lately, we'd been talking more about the future than about the present.

I got into the car feeling undeniably special and looking forward to what I thought was on tap for the evening: dinner at our favorite Thai restaurant. As usual, we began chatting away. I was so engrossed in our conversation that it was some time before I realized that we were in a completely unexpected part of the city, heading in the opposite direction from the restaurant. For the first time that evening, I paused.

"Nick?" I asked. "Are we lost?"

He smiled knowingly. "Just sit back and relax," he said. "I've got a surprise."

My heart began to race with a deep and sudden anxiety. Where were we going? Why was Nick doing this? Didn't he know I hated surprises? I edged back in my seat, my back tight, shoulders rigid, arms braced. There was no rational reason for me to feel as I did, but I couldn't help it. Mentally, I understood that Nick simply wanted to do something special. Even so, I couldn't shake the familiar dread and fear that surprises had brought out in me for as long as I could remember.

I glanced over at Nick. I could tell from the way he'd set his jaw that he was frustrated by my response. A minute later, he turned the car around and drove back the way we'd come.

After a few minutes of tense silence, Nick slowed the car and turned to me. "Christine," he said, eyes piercing and tone lowered, measuring each word. "This exact same thing keeps happening in so many different ways. I don't want to just ignore it. We need to talk, and we need to talk now. We're headed back to your place."

I swallowed hard. Nick had never spoken to me this way. It unsettled me—and made me feel even *more* anxious because I'd upset him! And I definitely didn't want to explain to him why surprises tended to make me so tense. I tensed even more, dreading the conversation I'd spent most of my life avoiding.

Nick pulled into my driveway. He wasted no time getting to the point—we were still sitting in the car when he said, "Christine, I'm on your side. I'm not trying to hurt you. But for some reason, anytime I try to do something spontaneous, or anytime it seems as if things are slipping out of your direct control, you freak out. Then if I try to talk to you about it, you put up walls and shut me out emotionally. I don't know what's going on, but it's clear that you don't trust me, and if this relationship isn't based on trust, then what are we doing?"

I knew he was right as soon as the words came out of his mouth. I loved him. I did. But I didn't *trust* him completely. It had nothing to do with his character or anything he'd done.

The fact was, I didn't trust *anyone* completely.

In a softer tone, he added, "You know I love you. But I can't shake the feeling that you're waiting for me to do something to disappoint you or hurt you—which I inevitably will—so you can have an excuse to end this. I want this to work out between us, Christine, but I need you to trust me—or there's really no point in going any further."

This was not the first time Nick had challenged my defensive posture. In fact, throughout our relationship, Nick had chipped away at many of the defenses I'd used to keep others at arm's length—mostly simple things, like not allowing him to open doors for me, or carry a box. Fiercely independent, I insisted on doing things for myself. Nick was the first person to stick around long enough to break through my defenses. His gentle persistence at doing and fixing things for me was a new experience, but I gradually gave in to his help. In the process, he won my heart—just not all of it. There was a piece I hung onto yet.

Now Nick was fighting for that piece too. He was calling me out of the fortress I'd built to protect myself. In my head, I understood that we couldn't move ahead as a couple if I didn't let him into my confidence, my trust. I *wanted* to be more open and trusting. But there was a barrier to that openness—a barrier I had no confidence I could ever overcome, and a great dread of trying.

My heart pounded. My palms sweated. My tongue felt like lead wrapped in paper. I couldn't seem to form words, and thought that if I tried, the only sound likely to come out would be a croak. I could take the easy way out—get out of the car and walk away. Keep the protection I'd built around my heart and soul. But if I did that, I would lose him. I sat there, wavering. Stay behind all my protective barriers and keep silent? Or reveal what I'd hidden behind them?

It wasn't a new dilemma. For months, I'd spent half the time wanting to share everything with Nick about my past—

and the other half positive that I wanted to never mention it. Wasn't my past just the past? Did I really need to tell him? Hadn't I already dealt with it? If I told him, would he think it was my fault? Would he wonder why I'd never said anything? Would he question why I hadn't found a way to stop it sooner? Would he want someone untouched?

All the hurt I'd hidden — yet still felt — for years welled up inside. I'd thought I had dealt with it, resolved it, put it to rest. But now those old wounds threatened to reopen at any moment.

I looked up at Nick, and that one look resolved my dilemma. Seeing the bewilderment on his face was like looking in a mirror, seeing the confusion I'd seen on my own face for so many years. For both of our sakes, I had to bring it out of the darkness and into the light.

I took a deep breath. "I do love you. I *want* to trust you ... it's just not that easy for me." *How to say it? How to tell?* I breathed deeply again and, sitting there in the driveway, began to tell him how I had been abused for many years as a girl, by several different men. When I said the word *abused*, I started to shake. Telling the man I loved what other men had done to me was the hardest thing I had ever done.

As I spoke, I couldn't look at Nick. I looked at the floor of the car and poured out what I'd kept secret for years, things that had become unspeakable to me. And once I'd breached the dam, there was no holding anything back — it came out in a flood. *If I'm going to lose you over this, Nick,* I thought, *then you may as well know it all.* All the hidden things came pouring out: places, incidents, memories I hadn't even known I had — but one led to another, a narration of horror that shocked us both.

Finally, I stopped. Nick had not once interrupted. I had not once looked up, and now I felt completely exposed, vulnerable, spent. And yet, though I know it sounds clichéd, I also felt a great weight lifted off me. For the first time, I felt a freedom I hadn't even known I lacked.

UNEARTHING THE BURIED HEART

But now the die was cast. There was no going back. I could no longer run. The past had caught up with me, and God was using this man I loved dearly to force me to deal openly with all the secrets.

And they hadn't been secrets just from the rest of the world. Even I had been amazed by the power of my emotional response to reliving those years of abuse. It was clear that there was much I had not admitted to myself: that I was still afraid of what had happened to me, and shamed by the abuse. I still felt guilt. My heart had been broken and trampled. I'd thought that the part I'd hung onto had been healed. But now I knew that it wasn't healed at all. I had simply put a Band-Aid over a gaping wound, hoping that it would mend itself and go away. I said I loved God with my whole heart ... only my heart wasn't whole. It was broken and bruised and in pieces. I had vowed to never let anyone ever again hurt, betray, use, or abuse me. I hadn't realized that, by locking myself behind these walls, I was also locking out love. Now, through Nick, God was helping me confront a question I'd not reckoned with: Why didn't I believe that the miracle God could work in other hearts he could work in mine as well?

"Oh Nick," I said, "I so want to trust you, but at a certain point I can't seem to help but pull back to protect myself. Those men who hurt me were supposed to be men I could trust. I *did* trust them. My family did too. But they didn't prove trustworthy. And when one of them would move out of my life, and there would be a period when the abuse would stop, I would let down my defenses, thinking I had a chance to start over. Then the abuse would start again—an endless cycle. I learned it was safer to keep up my guard all the time than to trust anyone even some of the time."

The walls were crumbling now. "I feel pulled apart inside," I confessed. "I want to give you the key to the innermost recesses of my heart, but I don't know where I last put it. The frustrating thing is: You won't go! I know it sounds strange, but if by holding you at arm's length and failing to trust you, I can influence you to leave, then I've proven that I'm really not worth staying with—and so I can just give up, because there's no real hope. If you stay, I'm forced to ask myself, *Is there actually something in me that makes me worth his time and sacrifice?*

Nick reached over and held me for the longest time. "I'm so sorry that ever happened to you," he said. "I'm just so sorry."

I sat there motionless in his arms. *Did his heart really hurt that much for me? Did he love me so much that he felt a part of my pain? Did he really wish that he could somehow make it all better?* I was surprised. Nick now knew about my past—my secrets and shame and guilt—and he wasn't pushing me away as I'd anticipated. In fact, quite the opposite—he was pulling me closer. He still loved me. Knowing all that he now knew, he seemed to love me even more.

I felt a stirring inside. It was my fragmented and wounded heart beginning to be restored. Through Nick's earthly love for me, God was showing me a glimpse of his great divine love.

DELIVERED BUT NOT FREE

For more than twelve years, I had been wounded by abuse. All that pain had made me seal away a part of my heart and soul in what I thought was a safe, protected place. I desperately craved close relationships, but feared them too—because I never wanted to be hurt again. I had become trapped.

An overbearing boss crushes your spirit. An unfaithful spouse betrays your trust. Cruel friends trample your heart with spiteful words. Insensitive parents strip your confidence. Unthinking teachers call you stupid and tell you that you will never amount to anything, squashing your self-worth. Rebellious children stomp all over you. Abusers try to take your soul. Whatever the source of the attack on our bodies, souls, and spirits, the hurt stings and the damage goes deep.

You remember the exact moment of the damage—how the earth seemed to stop spinning, how your world came to a halt. You can't forget the sights, smells, a song playing, what you wore, who else was there. These things freeze in memory, and a part of you freezes with them, forever stuck in that place, unable to move on.

You may be delivered from your situation, but you are not free.

That was true for me. Though I was no longer in bondage to my abusers every day, I had shuttered my heart. I didn't trust anyone, not even God. I kept him at a distance by giving him my time, but not all of myself. I didn't trust him to take care of me any more than I trusted Nick.

I couldn't forgive the men who hurt me, nor myself for being abused. Worse, I realized that I hadn't forgiven God. Where was he, after all, when I was a helpless child and those men laid hands on me? Why didn't he stop them?

Did I really think that? How could I compel others to love God with their whole hearts when I kept a part of my own from him? How could I move, undaunted, into an unknown future with a God I did not trust?

Although I was shocked by this revelation, God was not. Since he knows everything, he knew that if I were to be truly free, I needed to deal with this wound. He was able to heal me—but I had to *choose* that healing. If I were to be made whole, first I had to admit that I wasn't. I had to accept that I needed help. I needed to reach up to God and out to others as part of the healing exercise of a whole heart. Only then could I purely love others. Especially Nick.

BOUND BY SCAR TISSUE

When life hurts us, we want the quick fix, instant newness, wholeness. We want God to fix the problem. But most often, damage doesn't happen overnight—and neither does healing.

Some wounds heal over, but scar tissue remains. Complete healing takes time and goes deep, into painful places.

Once, on a risky jump down a ski slope, I ruptured major ligaments that connect the bones in the knee. I needed emergency surgery. Afterward, as the doctor unwrapped the dressing for that first post-op look, he warned me that my leg would look abnormal due to the swelling.

Still, I was shocked. My leg was covered in blood stains, and there were tubes coming out of my knee to drain fluids, creating a futuristic, robotic, Borg-like appearance.

The doctor noticed my anxiety. "Don't panic," he said. "This is perfectly normal, given the trauma of the surgery. Give it time, and your leg will return to normal."

"If it doesn't, I'm going to have to wear trousers for the rest of my life," I joked.

The doctor smiled. He pulled up a chair to sit next to my bed. "You're obviously a highly motivated person and want to get back to normal as soon as possible," he said. "Your enthusiasm is admirable, but you need to remember that recovery from this kind of surgery won't be easy. You'll have to push through considerable pain to regain strength and range of motion in your leg."

Well, that was discouraging. Still, I was determined to be his fastest-healing patient. "I'll be running along the beach in no time," I said, smiling weakly. "I hate pain, but if it's only temporary, I'll push through it. I'll bear it."

He looked sympathetic. "I should warn you," he said, "that the pain of the recovery will be much greater than the pain of the injury."

He explained: Scar tissue had developed from my initial trauma and then the further trauma of surgery. As my body attempted to heal itself, protective fibers grew around the injured ligaments. My range of motion, circulation, and even sensation in that leg were affected. Unless those protective fibers of scar tissue were broken down, I would never regain full range of motion; I might even have to wear a leg brace the rest of my life. The only way to break down the scar tissue would be an ongoing process of rehabilitation with a good physical therapist and unrelenting commitment on my part.

With that, the doctor wished me the best and walked out.

I lay there trying to digest all that I'd heard. I'd thought the surgery was going to fix all of my problems. Now I'd learned that it had been just the beginning of an extremely painful process leading, I hoped, to full recovery. My choices were limited. I could avoid the pain and live with a partially functioning leg for the rest of my life, or I could embrace the pain and experience a full recovery.

The scar tissue in my knee is no different than the scar tissue in our hearts. Years of haunting memories after abuse or an attack of any kind can last longer than the actual events. The heart broken in an instant when you learn of an adulterous affair can keep you from loving for years, if ever again. The harsh names you're called on the schoolyard as a child can echo in your ears the rest of your life.

So many things can injure us, break our hearts and spirits, wound our souls and change us forever, leaving our heart overlaid with fibers of mistrust, bitterness, self-condemnation, guilt, fear — all the things that keep us from stepping out, risking, moving ahead.

We want God to fix us and heal us quickly and without pain. But when that doesn't happen, we're left flat on our backs or limping or wearing a brace. And here is the tragedy: *We have no strength of spirit or wholeness of heart to set anyone else free because we are not free or healed ourselves.*

But God promises us that his plans for us are for good and not for evil, to prosper us and not harm us, plans to give us a future and a hope (Jeremiah 29:11).

Have you been wounded? Is your heart shattered, covered with scar tissue? God has a great plan for your future, but if you have not dealt with the wounds of your past, you will not be able to go where he is calling you to go.

Hurting people hurt other people in turn. I was hurt—and because of that, I had hurt Nick and who knows how many others. If I were to stop hurting and instead find wholeness and healing, then I needed to forgive and trust. Yes, I needed to forgive those who had abused me. But I also needed to go further: I needed to trust Nick who loved me, and I needed healing in my relationship with God.

I grappled with this idea for weeks after the confrontation in my driveway with Nick. I read and reread Jesus' promise that if you forgive others their sins, your heavenly Father forgives you, but if you do not forgive others their sins, neither will your Father forgive your sins (Matthew 6:14–15).

How could I forgive such a thing as repeated abuse? How could I forgive God for my trust being broken so repeatedly as a child?

STEPS TOWARD WHOLENESS AND HEALING

It's hard for someone who is supposed to have it all together to admit that he or she needs help. But that's exactly what I had to do. I was teaching students how to trust God in their daily walk, and now I had to learn to do that myself, all over again.

My questions were so big that I took them to a counselor. Though the confrontation with Nick had pounded the fortress around my heart, there was a wall left. I would never be free from the haunting memories and old feelings of shame, self-condemnation, anger, bitterness, and mistrust, until I determined to make new memories and embrace new feelings such as peace, kindness, and compassion.

In the same way, the wife whose husband has left her cannot be free to love again if she is stuck in bitterness toward him. The boy whose coach scolds mercilessly cannot be free to push himself to new limits if he's just focused on past "failings." The child whose parents never encouraged can never find hope while replaying old mental tapes of what's not possible in life. Freedom and wholeness start within.

God tells us to bear with one another and forgive one another just as we've been forgiven (Colossians 3:13). *Bearing* means there will be pain to endure. The healing process ahead of me would take the touch of God's hand, as well as deliberation and work, and no sip of elixir or pill I could pop would take that away. I needed to work through the emotional scar tissue, just as I'd worked through the pains of physical therapy.

Healing doesn't happen overnight. The Bible tells the story of Naaman, a valiant captain who was stricken by leprosy (2 Kings 5:1–19). He was told to dip seven times in the muddy Jordan River in order to be healed. He couldn't go to a prettier river with cleaner waters and just dip once. He had to get in the Jordan and bathe there again and again and again—seven times. Healing was a messy process, a choice he had to make. It works the same in our lives.

We have to choose to heal, and trust that if we do what God, the Great Physician, asks—if we forgive those who have wounded and damaged us—there will be a change, a good result, strength and wholeness.

That means we can:

- **Forgive every time we feel anger or mistrust or bitterness.** Instead of dwelling on the emotions that were eating me alive, I had to forgive. For years I'd thought that forgiving meant I was letting my abusers off the hook. But my refusal to forgive them was doing more damage to me than to them. Not forgiving is like ingesting poison and expecting it to kill someone else. Unforgiveness keeps us cowardly and stunted, isolated and alone, ugly and bitter. Jesus said to forgive seventy times seven (Matthew 18:22) because no matter how much you forgive others, he has forgiven you even more (Colossians 3:13). When the anger returns, when the pain resurfaces, when we don't want to forgive again, we must remember how much God forgave us.

- **Stay in the present moment or think on the future,** instead of rehearsing old injustices and letting our lives revolve around the past. There's greater reward in replacing our negative thoughts with what is pure and noble and lovely (Philippians 4:8) now—and in the future. But we have a hard time thinking that way; we naturally default to what's negative or in the past. Just as physical therapy was required to break down scar tissue, I needed to stretch and strain my mind and heart "to take hold of that for which Christ Jesus took hold of me" (Philippians 3:12). Christ took hold of me to give me, and all of us, a new destiny—to make a difference in this world for him. The only way we can claim that destiny is to let go of our past and look ahead (Philippians 3:13–14) to a heavenward future.

- **Let others make their own choices, and let go of the illusion of control.** We often try to control and manipulate the circumstances and the people around us. We are not in control; God is. He is sovereign (2 Samuel 7:23). This meant I could allow Nick to make decisions without questioning every one, or feeling the need to control him when we were together. He could choose a restaurant without consulting me—even, I chuckled to myself, a restaurant not of my choosing.

- **Stop trying to punish with anger and hate those who hurt us. Instead, we can let God deal with them.** If we're building walls to protect ourselves, we're just keeping God and others out. We think we'll get back at someone back through anger or by ignoring them. God wants us to drop it. He knows we are hurt (Isaiah 49:13). He won't just let things go. We don't have to deny our pain, but we have to let go of our need to pay back. God will contend on our behalf (Psalm 35:1), but it is usually not how we would do it. He's got our back.

- **Trust in God instead of ourselves.** Proverbs 3:5–6 says to trust the Lord with all your heart and lean on him, rather than on your own understanding, because he will direct your path. His name is trustworthy (Psalm 20:7). I saw how God guided the Israelites to the Promised Land, how he brought people—like the wise men, and even the misguided, like Paul—to Jesus. What he did for others, God could do for me, if I would only trust him and follow his leading.

- **Believe our wounds can make made us stronger.** I couldn't heal my own heart any more than I could wish my knee back to its full strength and power without the guidance of a great physical therapist. The surgeon who operated on my knee later told me that after therapy my right leg, the one that had been injured, was stronger than my left. The hard work of returning that leg to "normal" had strengthened the muscles and connective tissue. In the same way, the wounded part of my heart was strongest as well. God steps in and promises to be strong when we are weak (2 Corinthians 12:10).

Beyond the things we can do, God is at work too. God—Great Physician that he is—is always good. He can always be trusted. He is in the business of turning anything bad into everything good.

In the Bible, Joseph is abused by his brothers and sold into slavery, then repeatedly scarred and neglected by his enemies. But Joseph made an amazing discovery, revealed to us in Genesis 50:20:

You intended to harm me, but God intended it for good to accomplish what is now being done, the saving of many lives.

What Joseph found to be true then is no less true for us today: Anything meant in this world for evil, God can use for good. God is able to take the mess of our past and turn it into a message. He takes our trials and tests and turns them into a testimony.

The enemy meant evil against me when he allowed those men to abuse me, just as he meant evil against me when I was left unnamed and unwanted at a hospital. But God took what was meant for ill and turned it into good. Romans 8:28 does not say that all things that happen to us are good, but it does say that God is able to work all things together for the good of those who love him and are called according to his purpose.

If we trust him with our broken and wounded hearts, he will bring healing, restoration, and wholeness. He takes the weak, the marginalized, and the oppressed and makes all things new. What someone else would leave for broken, he sees as beautiful. He cherishes that broken life, and loves, chooses, and heals to make it whole.

MY PAST COULD GIVE SOMEONE ELSE A FUTURE

Because I was willing—not necessarily able, but willing—to take one step and then another, and another, God has brought me to the most interesting places. He took what I thought was broken and unworthy—my heart—and made it into something beautiful by giving it to others who are flattened by life and circumstance. This is God's nature. The very thing that the enemy uses to try to destroy your life is the very thing God uses to help others. God can heal every hurt and can turn your scars into signs of strength for his glory.

Your past mistakes, hurts, and pain can help give someone else a future. Whatever we have gone through enables us to help others. God doesn't waste one experience of our lives. He uses everything to help someone else. He doesn't want us to remain crippled, immobilized, or paralyzed by the past. Instead, he sent us Jesus to show us how to step into the future.

I have always known that I was not the only one carrying around such pain. We are all broken in some way. We all have wounds. Some of us use that as an excuse to do nothing, to serve no one, but rather to sit and nurse our misery. That's not what God wants, and not the model we see over and over again in the Bible. The biblical model is that God deliberately chooses imperfect vessels—those who have been wounded, those with physical or emotional limitations. Then he prepares them to serve and sends them out *with their weakness still in evidence*, so that his strength can be made perfect in that weakness. In fact, more often than not, it's our weakness that makes us capable of serving, because those we serve identify with our pain. As always: God works *in* us so that he can work *through* us. And so he did with me.

I am so glad God used Nick to begin a process of healing and restoration in my heart. I never imagined that all the fears from my past that had paralyzed me for years could be used to give me courage to float. But that is just what happened, and on March 30, 1996, I walked into my future.

Nick was there, up ahead at the end of the aisle. With each step, I marveled at our good God, who had brought Nick into my life, then led him to turn the car around and stop and confront me with the truth. Each step that brought me closer to Nick also reminded me how God, by healing my heart, had come close to me.

I died so that you may be free, whole, restored, healed, he whispered. He had taught me over the last year of that healing process not to settle for anything less. My past no longer defined me or my future. I was whole to be loved and to love in return—to reach out for others' hands just as God had reached out for mine.

God whispered now, as he had been whispering, though I hadn't always heard it:

You are worth it.

As I came to the head of the aisle, Nick reached out and took the hand I held out to him, open and free, whole and healed.

"I'm so glad you actually came," he whispered in my ear.

Those words have echoed in my mind so many days since then. And the words I said to Nick in return are the same words I say to the wounded and scarred ones that the Great Physician brings me on the path of service he has set before me: *I wouldn't miss this for the world.*

chapter 5

Heartbreak — or Breakthrough?

I sat, relaxed and happy, in the chair in the examining room as Dr. Kent, my gynecologist, reviewed my chart. "You're twelve weeks and six days pregnant today, Christine," he said finally. "We should definitely be able to hear the baby's heartbeat. Why don't you lie on the table, and I'll go get the Doppler."

As he strode out, leaving the door open, I tried to get up on the table. At five-foot-three, I often have to stretch and reach for things, but this was ridiculous. *Why do they make these tables for six-foot-tall women?* I wondered. *Where's my pole for vaulting when I need it?* I could see a woman in the outer room trying not to laugh as she watched me. After several attempts, laughing at how ridiculous I must look, I conceded defeat and used the step to get up onto the table. *Some day*, I told myself, lying down, *I will be a lady. Just not today.*

Waiting for Dr. Kent's return, I thought back to one of the first times I'd been on this very table, in this very room. It seemed like just yesterday. *Yet had it really been more than two years?* Having a baby blurs all sense of time. *Where does it go?*

I wondered. How quickly my life had changed with a child. I couldn't remember when I last slept through a whole night, or finished an entire meal, or watched a television show that wasn't on the Nickelodeon Junior channel for kids. And I wouldn't change a thing. I loved having a little girl, and couldn't wait for this baby's birth. The joy that Catherine had brought into my life was about to double! I couldn't have been happier, or more excited: Today I would get to hear my new baby's heartbeat!

I remembered that the first time I'd heard Catherine's tiny heart beating I was shocked. It sounded out of control, like galloping horses. I'd panicked! "What's wrong?" I'd blurted to Dr. Kent. "Why is the baby's heart racing?"

That galloping sound was perfectly normal, he'd reassured me. "Your baby is healthy."

At least now I knew what to expect. Still, the sound would be like hearing a miracle all over again, a growing life inside my womb. *What a wonder God created when he allowed women to carry life. What a mystery and a privilege.* The weeks of morning sickness, the last three months of discomfort, all seemed suddenly small compared to this momentous event, the first sound to my ears of the living, breathing human being inside me.

Dr. Kent came back into the room holding a brand-new Doppler unit. "We just got this yesterday. I can't wait to try it," he said, ripping open the plastic packaging. I braced myself as he applied the cold gel on my stomach. I never liked this part. That gel was so icy and sticky. Seeing my discomfort, Dr. Kent tried to work fast. He began to move the Doppler from side to side. I waited for the soothing sound of the galloping horses. I knew from experience that it could take a few minutes for the Doppler to pick up anything, because the baby could be sleeping or lying at an awkward angle.

Dr. Kent seemed very focused. I squirmed just slightly and grew impatient. More slowly, more deliberately, he moved the instrument across my stomach.

This baby sure likes to sleep, I thought. *It must be a boy for sure, because we could hear Catherine's heart beating right away.* She was always moving, kicking, or punching me. I smiled, but Dr. Kent seemed even more focused. He continued moving the instrument, more slowly now, in wider circles across my stomach.

I remained quiet. I didn't want to miss that first beat.

Finally, he stopped and looked me in the eye. "Christine," he said, "I can't find a heartbeat."

STUNNED

No heartbeat? Before he could add anything, I blurted, "Then something must be wrong with your brand-new Doppler. Try a different one."

I couldn't read Dr. Kent's thoughts from his expression as he called his assistant to bring him the old Doppler equipment. He seemed emotionless and simply intent. Neither of us spoke as he applied more gel to my stomach and began the search again. This time the gel felt even icier as I waited for the sound of life. *Wake up, little one. C'mon. Time to wake up.*

After several quiet minutes, Dr. Kent asked me to get up. "I'm going to arrange for an ultrasound immediately," he said, all joviality gone from his voice. He picked up the phone to personally call the clinic. I shivered as I heard him say, "And could you make this one a priority?"

The look on his face and tone in his voice alarmed me. This was serious.

I offered up a hasty, heartfelt prayer: *Oh God, please, please let everything be okay with my baby. Let this just be some kind of mix-up. You gave Nick and me this child. Let the ultrasound show the baby simply sleeping at a strange angle. Okay, Lord? Please?*

As I hurried out of Dr. Kent's office, I decided to walk to the clinic, just two blocks away. I needed the fresh air—and besides, I could call Nick instead of concentrating on driving and finding parking. I needed to hear his voice, even though I knew he would be in the middle of total mayhem at the office.

As I expected, his "hello" and patient listening steadied me. In a rush, I told him what was happening. "Chris," he said gently, "everything is going to be fine. You are going to have the ultrasound and the baby will be okay. I'm so sorry I'm not there to go through this with you. Call me right away with the good report." He prayed for us just as I arrived at the clinic, then we said good-bye.

I took a deep breath as I opened the door. With that quick walk and prayer, I felt comforted, loved, and reassured. *There's just been some mistake. This test will clear up everything*, I thought. *The ultrasound will show a perfect and healthy growing baby in my womb.*

At the front desk, I was given a clipboard loaded with forms. I hurriedly answered all the questions, eager to get on with the test. *God*, I prayed again, *thank you for being with me*. I handed the clipboard back to the clerk.

In short order, a nurse brought me to the room set up for ultrasounds, where the technician, Jane, asked me to lie down on the table while she read over Dr. Kent's notes, which had already been forwarded. When she looked up, I couldn't help but notice how deliberately she avoided making eye contact. *Don't read anything into that*, I told myself. *She is simply preoccupied with her job. Everything will be fine.*

I held completely still as she started the ultrasound. She moved the device slowly, intently, across my stomach, soon becoming fixated on one spot. As she steadied the device in that one area, she studied the computer screen intently. I tried to see what she was seeing, but nothing looked recognizable, just a gray screen or wavy lines and dots. She spent several minutes measuring, over and over, that particular spot of my stomach, highlighting it from many different angles — and never saying one word. I kept still and silent.

Finally, she stopped. "Mrs. Caine," she said, and it struck me as so formal after the friendliness of my conversation with Dr. Kent. "If you look at the lower left corner of the screen, you will see the fetus."

Fetus? The word always threw me. I never referred to Catherine as a fetus. Neither had Dr. Kent. *This is my baby,* I wanted to say, *not a "thing," not something abstract. This is a new-growing person.* I tried to focus instead on what she was saying.

"Your records show that you are almost thirteen weeks pregnant, but the fetus is the size of an eight-week-old. This ultrasound indicates that the fetus stopped growing almost five weeks ago. There is no sign of a heartbeat. I am so sorry to have to tell you that it is no longer alive."

It? No longer alive?

"It is dead," she said, just like that.

Dead? I shook my head slightly in unbelief, totally stunned and devastated. I couldn't take my eyes off the screen. *How could this have happened?* Nick and I had prayed for this baby every day. We believed this little one was from God, given for a specific purpose and destiny. We had plans and hopes, dreams and expectations. Since we thought our baby must be a boy, we had, with excitement and love, narrowed down our choice of names to our favorites: Daniel Joseph or Jackson Elliott. *Our baby couldn't be dead! Wouldn't I have known? Wouldn't God want this new life he'd given to grow and serve him? Didn't he know how excited Nick and I were to have another baby? God wouldn't let this happen to us.*

Jane left the room as I buttoned up my shirt and collected myself to leave. Alone, I thought of all the shoulda, coulda, wouldas: *Maybe I should have planned to have children earlier. Thirty-seven is late. The older you get, the greater the risk. Perhaps I could have avoided this if I'd stopped traveling. All the time zones, the changes in food, climate, and water, the lack of rest—those things had to have taken a toll on my body. What else might I have done wrong? Is this a judgment for some sin in my life?*

The questions spun as, numbly, I left the clinic, full of disappointment and sadness. I had walked into Dr. Kent's office that morning filled with life, hope, excitement, and dreams. I had expected to have a routine checkup, then leave and get back to the work I loved with Nick.

Now I just wanted to be alone. I didn't want to talk to anyone or explain anything. I found a quiet corner outside and sat. I didn't even have the strength to cry. Never had the idea occurred to me that I might not carry this baby to full term.

For a long time I sat alone, heartbroken and bitterly disappointed. I prayed: *How could this have happened, God? What am I supposed to do with all the dreams Nick and I have for this child? Why did you give us this baby, just to take him away before we could even hold him, call him by name, or listen to his heartbeat and his cry and his laugh? How am I going to tell Nick? How will we tell others?*

Nick and I had made the announcement to our friends and family around the world as soon as I'd hit the eleven-week mark of confirmed pregnancy. Now I dreaded reliving the pain every time I conveyed the sad news to someone else.

We had spent an entire year thinking and praying about another child, hoping for a playmate for Catherine and figuring it might take a while for me to get pregnant because of my age. We were so surprised when it hadn't taken long at all, and the age gap between Catherine and our next baby seemed perfect. We had already adjusted our work schedules and commitments for the next year so that I could stop traveling for a while, and we had even planned the nursery room in our home.

Catherine. How would we possibly tell our sweet little Catherine? Though just a toddler, she understood that she was going to get a baby brother or sister soon, and she was so delighted, so thrilled. We talked about it all the time. How could she possibly understand?

I was heartbroken not only for me, but for Nick and Catherine and everyone in our lives.

THE BIG DEAL OF DISAPPOINTMENT

Disappointment is a sad and terribly lonely place. We all land there at some point in life. Your children move away and never call. Colleagues betray you. The company to which you've devoted your years "downsizes," and you're on the list right along with the newcomer and the slacker. The man you love doesn't love you back. The perfect child you dream over and tend in pregnancy is born with defects that will make the rest of your life, and all your family members' lives, nothing less than challenging. You get a disease or suffer an injury for which there is no relief or cure. Your investments dwindle. Friends disappear. The one you've prayed to find Jesus never does. Your dreams shatter. Best-laid plans go astray. Other Christians fail you. People disappoint you. You even disappoint yourself.

Any one of these things can introduce sadness, discouragement, and dismay into your life; any of these things can daunt you. And the long series of disappointments you accumulate in a lifetime can stop you from moving forward into all the goodness God has planned for you — and that means they'll be stopping not only you, but also all those God has destined you to reach along your life journey. After all, how can anyone stuck in their own disappointment help others out of theirs? How can you convince others of the wonder of God's promises if you doubt them yourself? How can you share how God has saved you when you don't feel saved at all?

I had to resolve my own heartache if I expected to keep ministering to others in theirs.

But this would be a hard one to move beyond. Why is it that you can know in your head that God has your good in mind and can redeem any and every circumstance, and yet you can still feel hugely disappointed and deeply despondent? Your head tells you God is trustworthy — but in a moment of aching disappointment, your heart tells you he's not even there.

In my world and Nick's, after the miscarriage, everything was not okay. If we were going to get through this without developing bitterness of spirit, we had to process our disappointment in a healthy way. We had to conclude for ourselves that the valley of death we were walking through isn't, to borrow an image from *Pilgrim's Progress*, a Slough of Despond from which we would never emerge, but simply a shadow, and that shadow would not define our lives. Christ does.

And yet—this was not a job loss, or a financial reversal, or a wrecked car. This was the death of a long-awaited child, a child much-loved though I never had the chance to hold him in my arms or kiss his head or feel his breath on my face. This would be so hard to triumph over.

If I were to move beyond the daunting disappointment of this moment, I would have to remind myself of things about God that I knew to be true, though they might not feel true at the moment. There was so much I did not know, yet I was determined to cling to what I did know. I turned to the only place I could in such grief. I turned to God's Word.

Let me share with you the truths that brought me deep comfort and helped me begin to accept the disappointments that we cannot escape in life.

GOD'S PROMISES IN DISAPPOINTMENT

God Is Not Unfair, Silent, or Hidden

God knows things we don't know, and does things in ways we could never predict. He is infinite and we are finite. After all, God reminds us:

> *My thoughts are not your thoughts, neither are your ways my ways.... For as the heavens are higher than the earth, so are my ways higher than your ways and my thoughts than your thoughts. (Isaiah 55:8–9)*

The biblical book of Job tells us the story of a man of great wealth who, in a terrifying series of events, lost everything—his children, his wealth, even his health. Sitting in the dust, surrounded by men who had come to help him probe why such things had happened to him, Job lamented his losses and asked the great existential questions:

How many wrongs and sins have I committed?
 Show me my offense and my sin.
Where then is my hope—
 who can see any hope for me?
Though I cry, "Violence!" I get no response;
 though I call for help, there is no justice.
     (Job 13:23; 17:15; 19:7)

Job's friends spoke up then, offering him the world's wisdom, which helped him not at all. Finally God spoke—but even he did not answer Job's questions. Instead, he merely said that he was God, the great I AM, all-powerful and all-knowing, and that Job had no reason or right to question him. Job humbly repented—and God chose to restore all that Job had lost, and more.

And never, in the entire story, did God find it necessary to explain himself.

We will never understand, this side of heaven, why bad things happen to us and those we love. Nor will we understand so many unexplainable tragedies in this world, from war to famine to earthquake. But just because we do not understand these things doesn't mean we must stop trusting God, who has proven again and again that he loves us.

We, his creation, have no right to tell God how to express that love. We can know, for sure, that his choices will not be our choices. That is why faith says, along with Job, "Though he slay me, yet will I hope in him" (Job 13:15).

Is God unfair? Unjust? No—in fact, our very definitions of justice derive from God. Is he silent? He may choose not to speak to us directly—the psalmist often speaks of God's silence. And yet he has given us his Word, full of his messages for us, messages of love and reassurance. Is he hidden? "Those who seek me find me," he says in Proverbs 8:17.

Jesus Is with Us through Our Heartache and Leads Us to Something Better Ahead

Luke 24:13–35 tells of two disciples leaving Jerusalem after Jesus' burial. On the road to a town called Emmaus, they were heartbroken and bitterly disappointed. *How could God let this happen?* they wondered. *What should we do now?* They had hoped and believed that Jesus was the one sent to redeem Israel. But those hopes were shattered just as his body was shattered, and then beaten, bruised, crucified, and buried. Their dreams died on the cross with Jesus. Their work toward a new and better kingdom seemed over now, buried along with Christ. It had all been in vain.

A man met them on the road and walked along with them as they talked of these things. But they were so downcast, so crushed, they never took a good look at their fellow traveler. Their heads, like their hearts, were bent in despair.

"What are you discussing?" the man asked.

Amazed, they stopped. "Are you the only one visiting Jerusalem who does not know the things that have happened there in these days?" one of the men, Cleopas, said.

"What things?" the man asked.

"About Jesus of Nazareth," the men replied. "The chief priests and rulers handed him over to be sentenced to death, and they crucified him. We had hoped that he was the one who was going to redeem Israel. And what is more, it is the third day since all this took place."

It was then, when they looked up, that the man began explaining to them how Israel *was* going to be redeemed. He knew the promises of God by heart, and explained how those promises would be fulfilled in such a way that they would change the world. A new kingdom was at hand. Walking alongside him, the disciples listened. Before they knew it, they reached Emmaus, their destination. But the man started to continue on.

"Stay with us," the disciples urged.

He did, and when they all sat down to eat that night, at the table, he "took bread, gave thanks, broke it, and began to give it to them."

Jesus! Their eyes were opened. The one walking with them through their disappointment, the one who gave them hope that God had a plan, a plan so big that even a crucifixion couldn't stop it, a plan that would in fact use the crucifixion to redeem the world—was Jesus himself. He was not only alive but here, right in front of them, blessing them, feeding them, walking them through their deepest disappointment. He had not left them; he had not forsaken them.

How blinded we become by disappointment! Sometimes, like the disciples, we're so blind that we can't see Jesus walking with us through our heartache, leading us to something better ahead. He wants to show us that God has made a way for us that leads far beyond disappointment. God has big plans for us—things to do, people to see, places to go.

When we face disappointment, rather than wallowing in it, we can pray, *Lord, I don't understand why all this has happened. But I do know you want me to keep walking, keep looking for you, keep remembering that it's what I do with disappointment that matters. Help me, as you helped those on the road to Emmaus, to surrender both my memories of the past and my hopes for the future to you.*

Christ promises us that, beyond disappointment, something better awaits us. Some mission God designed just for us, custom tailored—something that takes us not on a road to nowhere but to a place where we can feed others just as he has fed us.

"Go," he told his disciples in Matthew 28:16–20. Go into all the world. Keep going past disappointment. Go and share everything I've shared with you. "And surely I am with you always, to the very end of the age."

Just as he blessed the disciples at the end of the hard road to Emmaus with the yeasty goodness of fresh-baked bread, he blesses us so that we can bless others—and then he invites us to accompany him further down that road, looking for others knocked off their feet by hurt and heartache.

STEPS TO OVERCOMING DISAPPOINTMENT

God knows when we need nurture and healing, refreshment and sustenance, and he gives us that. In fact, for our journey, he gives us five important tools to sustain us and to help us provide sustenance to others.

1. The Comfort in the Church

When you're hurting, going home is the best thing to do, and church is the believer's spiritual home.

The first Sunday after Nick and I lost our baby, taking that pain and disappointment to church seemed so counterintuitive. I knew that we would be surrounded by well-intentioned church friends asking, "How's the pregnancy going? How is the baby?" I dreaded having to answer those questions. But we knew that we needed to go to the House of God.

What I remember most about that Sunday is not how awful it was to answer people's questions about the baby and have to tell the news one more time, and again, and again, but rather how incredibly loving and warm our church family was to us. I had no idea how much I needed a loving community to share my burden. But God did. And as our church gathered 'round Nick and me in our grief, we were able to lift our eyes off our circumstances and see God's loving kindness.

2. The Power in Worship and Praise

I will never forget the moment on that Sunday when we began to sing "Blessed Be Your Name" by Matt and Beth Redman.[1] The lyrics pierced my heart:

> *Blessed be your name*
> *On the road marked with suffering*
> *Though there's pain in the offering*
> *Blessed be your name . . .*

I felt so empty when I began singing, but with each verse, I felt more and more emotion, and soon the tears came. The cry of the psalmist broke something in me and then filled my empty soul. The weight of my grief and the burden of feeling alone spilled out; peace and confidence in the Lord's love and care poured in. The words became my sacrifice, an offering to the Lord, who had already walked the road of suffering before me and now returned to meet me on it. I was in communion with him, knowing he wanted to bless me with "beauty instead of ashes, the oil of joy instead of mourning, and a garment of praise instead of a spirit of despair" (Isaiah 61:3). A spiritual exchange took place: I magnified the Lord instead of my disappointment. I began to remember his mercies more than my hurt.

3. The Strength in Choosing the Joy of the Lord

Joy and happiness are not the same thing. Happiness is based on circumstances. Joy is based on God. Happiness is rooted in positive emotions—and who doesn't like positive emotions? That's why we seek happiness. But joy is something more—it's a fruit of the Spirit (see Galatians 5:22–23), something that God divinely gives us through the power of his Holy Spirit.

Nothing about the circumstance of losing my baby made me happy. Not then, and not now. Yet God cared for me in that circumstance, and in every other circumstance before and since. He met me in that loss and walked me through it, because he had something good ahead to show me. That isn't happiness—but it's joy.

Joy isn't just "imitation happiness." It's something more. Think of happiness as the candy, the sweet. We all like sweets. But joy is like a medicine. When your heart is sick, when the pain seems unbearable—it's the medicine you want. Sweets just won't cut it.

"The joy of the Lord is my strength," we sing. And when we choose to serve God, we need to do so out of his strength. This takes joy.

Habbakuk 3:17–18 became his personal reminder to me: "Though the fig tree does not bud, and there are no grapes on the vines, though the olive crop fails and the fields produce no food, though there are no sheep in the pen and no cattle in the stalls, yet I will rejoice in the LORD, I will be joyful in God my Savior."

Because I had lost something precious, everything around me seemed dead. The circumstance was bad. But God is good—and like Habakkuk, I can rejoice in that.

4. The Wisdom of His Word

"How," you might ask, "can you rejoice when your heart is broken and you're hurting?"

When I learned that my baby had died, there was no escaping the pain—you can't stop the sorrow you feel. But feeling your disappointment and staying stuck in it are two different things. And the enemy wants you to stay stuck in disappointment. Disappointment is one of the tools in his toolbox, and it has a specific purpose: stopping you. God has incredible plans for you—and the enemy would like to keep you from ever experiencing them. God has promised to make all things new—and the enemy wants you to lose faith in that promise, and in the rest of God's promises.

But God's Word is full of his promises to us, and when we read it, we're reminded of them. The psalms, in particular, helped me through my heartache because in them are some of the most pure and honest heart cries ever written. Reading them gave me permission to admit that a dream had died, a hope had waned, and I had lost something very precious. Especially Psalm 61:1–2: "Hear my cry, O God; attend to my prayer. From the end of the earth I call to You, when my heart is overwhelmed; lead me to the rock that is higher than I" (NKJV). After the loss of our baby, I felt so overwhelmed that at times I didn't know what to pray. So I let the words of

David, who had walked this same path of grief before me, be my prayer and remind me that God still had a great plan and purpose for my life beyond my current disappointment.

The psalmist convinced me that this promise was meant for this earthly life. "I would have lost heart," he says, "unless I had believed that I would see the goodness of the LORD in the land of the living" (Psalm 27:13 NKJV). I meditated upon this idea day and night: I would see the goodness of the Lord in the land of the living because higher hands, God's hands, were at work. This gave me hope.

God has a plan and purpose for my life, as he does for each of us, beyond this moment of disappointment. We need not be passively resigned to the problems of life. We need not give up and stop fighting for what we believe in; there is always hope, and as long as there is hope, we can move forward—and bring others with us.

5. The Love of Family and Friends

My dear friend Kylie was like Jesus to me during my grieving time. She allowed me to express my disappointment, but not to wallow in it. She allowed me to talk about our family tragedy, but then nudged me not to dwell upon the sadness. Her nudges forced me to keep looking ahead, to focus not on what I had lost, but on all that I still had, and all that was still ahead. She knew that there was "a time to weep and a time to laugh, a time to mourn and a time to dance" (Ecclesiastes 3:4).

A friend will help you move forward through your disappointment and into God's promises. When you can't see anything but the fog of grief, a friend can help clear the way, help you laugh, bring a smile—and, like medicine, the mirth helps heal you. A friend will remind you that while there is still breath in your lungs, there is still hope—the promise of a new day. The psalmist reminds us: "Weeping may endure for a night but joy comes in the morning" (Psalm 30:5 NKJV).

THE APPOINTMENT IN DISAPPOINTMENT

For each of us, just as for the disciples walking unknowingly with Jesus as they headed to Emmaus, there is so much more waiting beyond disappointment. There are appointments that God has destined. There are good works for each of us to do. And isn't it interesting that the word *appointment* comes from within the word *disappointment*?

I've often marveled at that because I've seen again and again how disappointments take something from us: a dream, a piece of our heart—maybe whole chunks of it. But disappointments leave something too: a gift, an opportunity, a possibility to create change, to move from the valley of the shadow of death to new horizons, and to bring others with us on that road.

The enemy would like us to feel such a depth of disappointment that we never find our way back to the plan God has for us. If he can only convince us to stay stuck in our disappointment, we'll miss many of our future God appointments. And there are some disappointments that seem so big that we can't imagine ever being able to move beyond them. But the best way to get over your own broken heart or lost dream is to help others get over theirs. I discovered this to be true when I discovered that, because of the pain I'd endured after the loss of my own baby, I was able to help other women who had lost babies too.

Before my baby died, I had for years spoken at women's conferences and met women who'd lost a child before birth. I knew that one in four women experience a miscarriage, but that was just a number, a cold statistic. After my miscarriage, I understood what those women were feeling. Out of my own heartache and disappointment grew an even deeper sense of compassion for mothers of unborn children. The pain is real— yet often unacknowledged, invisible, because the mother never had a chance to hold the baby in her arms, to hear its heart beating next to hers. Now I, too, had experienced this invisible loss, and the heartache had been harsh and unforgettable. I would never look at such invisible yet profound pain the same way again. I would not be dismissive of the hurt someone else felt or expressed. Like any other wound, heartache takes time and attention and good medicine to heal. This is what God had given me—and I wanted to make sure that other bereaved mothers received time, attention, and spiritual and emotional medicine too.

Not all bereaved mothers, of course, lost their children before birth.

Maria is the director of our legal program for The A21 Campaign in Greece. A few years before I met them, Maria and her husband Dimitri were stunned when their fourteen-year-old son, their youngest child, was diagnosed with stomach cancer. Faithful servants of God who had served as pastors for more than twenty years, Maria and Dimitri and their family earnestly, diligently prayed for God to heal Peter. Peter was an extraordinary son—a leader among the youth who prayed for revival and transformation for his generation.

But Peter's healing was not to come this side of eternity.

My heart broke as I heard Maria's and Dimitri's story. I can only assume that having lost my baby before I could even hold him in my arms gave me only a glimpse of the agony they must have felt after watching their son grow for fourteen years.

Others were not so sympathetic, adding to Maria and Dimitri's pain. "Where is your God now?" some mockers asked. "Why didn't he heal your son, if he is so powerful, so good? He is not a good God. If he were, why would he take your fourteen-year-old when there are so many bad people walking the earth?"

Why indeed?

For some questions, there are no answers that make sense. When someone such as Peter dies, no explanation will satisfy the questions crying out inside. As with Job, our deepest questions go unanswered.

Maria and Dimitri didn't try to answer them. Instead, they determined to walk down that road of disappointment and heartbreak with Jesus. On the day of Peter's funeral, still burdened with pain, sorrow, and grief, their family made a decision. Even though they did not understand why this tragedy had occurred, they would continue to trust God. They would keep on believing his promises. They would look for other heartbroken travelers on that Emmaus road, and they would introduce them to a Savior who would walk it with them.

They proclaimed at the funeral:

Today is a sad day, but it is not a bad day. The devil thinks he has the victory because our son has died. But our son is alive with his Jesus, and is partying in heaven. The devil has not won. We are not burying our child today, but we are sowing him as seed into the soil of this nation. We believe in a mighty harvest of young people to spring forth. Out of one death, there shall arise new life.

Their words said, this family bruised by grief but beautiful with belief stood silently. All of those gathered around them kept silent too. What is to be said in the face of such faith?

The enemy would have liked such a deeply painful occasion to blind those gathered. But the light of Jesus in Maria and Dimitri, in a moment of what was expected to be agony, instead showed people a way ahead.

There is a road through disappointment. There is a way beyond the shadow of the valley of death. Disappointment is not an end but an opportunity for a divine appointment. One disappointment, or even more than one, does not mean that all the good works God ordained for you long before you were born are now impossible, ended, defeated. There are still many ahead of you, *beyond* the disappointment. Heartbroken yet undaunted, Maria used Peter's death to propel her into the next chapter of good works God had destined her for.

In the days that followed Peter's funeral, Maria resolved not to let her family's words fall on barren ground. She had not been able to keep alive her dying son Peter, but she could reach out to those whose lives had become a kind of death. When she learned of human trafficking in her own country, she began to walk into dark valleys and down hard roads to find the hurting, the heartbroken, the deeply disappointed with life.

She laid aside her dreams of being simply a loving mom to her own children and serving quietly in her own church, and chose to become a bridge to the Emmaus road. Some people, she knew, find that road only because of someone else, someone else who has buried their broken dreams beside it and sown the pieces of their broken heart. Then she trusted Jesus to bring the harvest.

Since Peter's death, Maria has been responsible for restoring the lives of hundreds of girls in Greece rescued from human trafficking. She has been a bridge over unfathomable oceans of grief. She lost a son, and he took with him a huge part of her heart. But that loss became the encouragement and the heart of her campaign to help others.

Many times I've talked with Maria about walking that road to Emmaus. We've discussed how disappointment brought us to places beyond our wildest imaginings, hard places where it would have been so easy to get stuck — but instead, Christ ran to meet us there. We've thanked him together for leading us to places where we share others' grief — and offer them grace instead. And every time, I've marveled at how Christ breaks us like bread and spreads the pieces of us to even more people — five thousand, ten thousand, more. And always, he is running to meet us, or walking through the valleys by our side.

Even when I cannot see him, I hear the beautiful gallop of God's heartbeat for humanity.

part 3

GOD KNOWS MY
FEAR

chapter 6

Love and Fear

Ladies and gentlemen, there is no need to panic."

Panic? I'd been doing just fine till the captain of our flight made that announcement. Nick and I had barely made ourselves comfortable on a flight from Chicago to Raleigh, North Carolina, when the captain said the P word. Definitely not what you want to hear at thirty thousand feet.

We'd been airborne only twenty minutes and nothing seemed out of the ordinary. Even so, the mere mention of the word changed everything. My heart started to race. Passengers all around gasped—followed by an eerie silence as we waited for the captain to continue.

"We are having trouble getting the landing gear up," he said. "Rather than continue on to Raleigh, we'll have to turn around and try to land in Chicago."

Try? That's another word you never want to hear in midair.

I gulped as I watched fear spread up and down the aisles. Some passengers began to bow their heads and audibly pray. Others started to cry. Flight attendant call buttons lit up the plane like a Christmas tree as people begged for more information.

I overheard one lady ask her husband, "Are we going to crash and die?"

A few years before, I would have been one of the panicked ones. In fact, I probably would have been the most distraught person onboard. But now, even though my heart was definitely beating faster and I could feel myself shift to a state of heightened awareness, I wasn't clutching the armrests or bracing myself against the seat, losing reason and confidence. I slipped my hand into Nick's, grateful for his ever-calm demeanor.

True to form, he began quietly praying for us—not in fear, but as if he were asking a blessing on the morning meal or thanking God for the beautiful day. He committed the pilot, passengers, and a safe landing to the Lord. Then he leaned into me and whispered in my ear, "We'll be fine, Chris. God has not brought us this far for it all to end like this. He is with us and has our backs. You don't need to be afraid of anything." With that, he squeezed my hand, reclined his seat, and closed his eyes. Within a few minutes, believe it or not, he gave every impression of having drifted off to sleep.

While I couldn't replicate Nick's complete calm, I relished it. Something powerful is transferred from one person to another when fear is not allowed to rule the heart. *Anyway,* I thought, *this is so typically Nick. While everyone else panics, he just sits back with rock-solid confidence in the goodness and protection of God, and trusts him.* Nick has been this way for as long as I've known him, able to live out the instruction of Paul to the Philippians to "be anxious for nothing, but in everything by prayer and supplication, with thanksgiving, let your requests be made known to God; and the peace of God, which surpasses all understanding, will guard your hearts and minds through Christ Jesus" (Philippians 4:6–7 NKJV). I was grateful for Nick's quiet strength and confidence, and thanked God for it, and wanted more of that same quality myself.

By nature, I'm the total opposite. Left to my own devices, if I'd been writing to the Philippians, I probably would have begun, "Be anxious for everything," because I struggle to simply cast my cares on the Lord. For me, there is nothing simple about complete, unquestioning trust, and I've wrestled with God over this much of my life. Even now, after decades of seeing how God never leaves nor forsakes us and always works all things together for good, I catch myself having to consciously choose to trust, having to constantly remind myself that he is with me always, even in situations like this one where, in fact, the danger is real and undeniable.

But now, in that hushed and tense plane, I wasn't wrestling. The passengers had no choice—they could do nothing but wait, hope, and pray that we would land safely in Chicago. I joined them—on high alert but not panicked, watchful but not wilting. I sat calmly next to Nick, still reclined peacefully with his eyes closed. I looked out the window onto a beautiful, clear night sky, lit by stars and tiny lights on the plane's wings, and prayed. I could smile at myself too.

God, I thought, thanking him, *how things have changed.*

WHERE FEAR TAKES YOU

I used to be one of those people who got on a plane only if there was no other option. If I could get somewhere by car, bus, train, bicycle, scooter, or foot, I would—anything to avoid boarding a big mass of metal expected to, beyond all logic, somehow stay up in the sky. On an airplane, turbulence would send my mind into every possible worst-case scenario, always ending with the engines stopping in midair and the plane falling off the radar to disappear somewhere over the ocean, or bursting into flames. The possibilities terrified me.

And, because my work required me to go from one end of the globe to another, this fear was a bit of a problem. I'd prayed for God to take me wherever people needed to hear the good news of grace, and he was honoring that prayer. He opened doors across the country and around the world for me to speak. I knew this was what he'd called me to do. Somehow, I had to get to these places.

To answer that calling meant that I had to go through the doors God opened. And since I lived in Australia—the Land *Far* Down Under—getting from there to most anywhere else in the world meant flying, plain and simple.

Only it wasn't so simple for me. I'd said *yes* to God—but if I were to make good on that commitment, God would have to do a work in me. Flying taxed my mind, body, and spirit. I would sit bolt upright, my hands wrapped around the armrests, gripping them the entire journey. Most flights were long anyway, since Australia is so far away from anywhere, but to me, those flights were not merely long, but endless and exhausting. They fatigued me. I would arrive at my destinations anxious and arrested by fear—hardly the state people hope for in a guest speaker.

My terror and anxiety would actually begin a week before leaving. I would break out in a sweat every time I even thought about getting on the plane. My heart would begin to race and my chest would tighten. I had to force myself to think about other things.

Things were no better once we landed. As I exited the plane and entered the airport terminal, my legs were like jelly and I felt disoriented. I remember once trying to hold a conversation with the person who picked me up from the airport, still so shaken by flying that I could barely utter a coherent sentence. I'm sure it was presumed that I suffered from jet lag, but the time zone differences were the least of the reasons for my exhaustion.

Finally, returning from one trip so drained by the emotional and physical energy required for fighting my fears, I decided I was through with this. I told God that although I wanted to go and help people, I could no longer face the pressure or endure the process of getting on an airplane. I would limit myself to going to places I could drive to. *I'm willing to go, Lord, as long as the transportation is on the ground, within my comfort zone. I'll go anywhere for you, as long as I don't have to fly.*

As long as . . .

Can you imagine? That was how I was talking to God, the God who left everything in heaven to come to us, the God who asks us to go and do likewise. *I will*, I said. *I can. I'm going—as long as . . .*

Fear Freezes You

Everyone fears something. Muggers lurking in dark alleyways. Losing your wallet—or, worse, your job, leaving you penniless. Automobile or airplane crashes. Bites from vicious animals. The sting of a poisonous insect. The ridicule of hecklers when speaking publicly. Rejection or disinterest upon meeting new people. Losing a child. Being abandoned by a loved one.

Some of us fear failing. Others fear success. "What if I stick my neck out and fail?" we say. Or, "What if the business gets too big too fast and I can't keep up or my customers see how little I really know or what an amateur I am?" The most potent factor in becoming daunted, by far, is fear.

Some fears are rational, such as the healthy fear of walking a tightrope above a canyon, where the chances of injury or death are unacceptably high. Other fears are not so rational, like one of my own—being in too small or tight a space, or being confined. It does me no good to reassure myself rationally that, just because the space is small, that doesn't mean the walls will collapse around me and suffocate me. Some fears are subtle, a general apprehension or worry, while others are dramatic, like dread and terror.

When you're young, you may fear imaginary beasts in the dark or the closet. The invisible but oh-so-real monsters of disease and death may be the things adults fear—or secrets being brought to light. For all ages, whether fear is subdued or strong, rational or irrational, the danger real or imagined, fear will always try to stop you, trip you up, and put your life on hold. Sometimes, just thinking about your fears can paralyze you.

Fear Makes You Miss Out on the Best in Life

When you allow fear to dictate how you spend your days, you allow life to pass you by.

You can't walk up a steep hill to see a beautiful sunset because of your fear of heights. You can't bring yourself to go to the party because of your fear of crowds. You don't join that Bible study because you fear having to read aloud after you were taunted for doing so long ago in school. You keep to yourself because you fear people will ridicule your size. You struggle with food for fear you'll gain weight. You don't date because you fear being rejected. You're so terrified of spiders and bugs that you've never ventured to dig in the soil and plant that vegetable or flower garden of your dreams. You go along with a decision at work that you don't believe in because you fear speaking up will set you at odds with the team or cost a promotion. You avoid commitments outside your home because you're afraid if you aren't with your teenager all of the time he or she might get involved in the wrong crowd. You marry the first person who asks you because you fear no one else ever will. You sleep with someone you're not married to because you fear that unless you do, he or she will leave you and you'll be alone.

When you let fear run your life, you close yourself off from anything that might hurt or cost or make you uncomfortable—including opportunities to serve God and claim his promises.

God calls you to serve with just what you have and just who you are—but because of fear of rejection, the homeless person on the street never receives the hope you were created to give. You don't allow yourself to consider the mission trip you would love to participate in because you fear the unknown in a faraway land. The victim of trafficking stays bound, never experiencing the freedom you could have made possible. Your neighbor dies alone, never receiving your visit. The mother at your son's football practice continues to drink every night because she has no one to talk to about her marriage problems.

You languish alone and broken, unfulfilled, never experiencing what you alone were made to do—simply because of fear.

"The thief comes only to steal and kill and destroy," Jesus warned (John 10:10). Fear is a thief like that. But, Jesus went on to promise, "I have come that they may have life, and have it to the full."

To the full.

LOVE ENOUGH TO BELIEVE

"Do you love me?" Jesus asked Peter (John 21:17). It's really a question for each of us.

If you love me, he was saying, *then look at me* (Matthew 14:22–33). *Keep your eyes on me.*

If you love me, follow me (Matthew 16:24).

If you love me, go and do likewise (Luke 10:37).

If you love me, feed my sheep (John 21:15–17). *Tend my lambs.*

For years I yearned for deliverance from my fears—but I wanted something more than the Lord's simple instructions to keep my eyes on him. Instead, I prayed fervently for him to remove my fears—especially my fear of flying. I demanded, "Why won't you just take this fear from me? After all, I'm getting on this plane for you!"

And God, in his tender mercy, sent me back to his Word. God "has not given us a spirit of fear, but of power and of love and of a sound mind" (2 Timothy 1:7 NKJV). He knows that fear will not get us through danger. But love can, and a sound mind will, and courage. Courage, after all, is not the absence of fear. It's the will to persevere even in the face of fear. God's power resides in us, but we're not always confident of that because we can't see it.

We *do* see the dangers—being too high off the ground, perhaps, or staring into the cold face of an enemy. So we doubt, we question—and we let fear take over.

When Jesus asks, *Do you love me?* he is also saying: *Then keep your eyes on me. Keep believing in what I have created you to do. Turn over to me your fear, and hold fast to faith in me. Replace that fear—fear that I did not give you—with the love, power, and sound mind that I have given you. Know that my presence is your antidote to fear.*

He knew that we would be afraid, that we would doubt. That's why he tells us again and again in the Bible, "Fear not." Three hundred and fifty times he tells us. Fear not. Fear not. Fear not. Fear not. When angels appeared to characters in the Bible, the first words they spoke were usually, "Fear not."

It's like a mother instinctively reaching for her child crying in the storm, wrapping her arms around the trembling heart, and soothing over and over, "It's okay. I'm here with you. Don't be afraid."

It's like the time Nick and I took the girls to an amusement park. They were so excited, and the thing Catherine was most excited about was playing on the gigantic trampoline—the kind where you are secured into a harness and then can bounce into the air, rise and twirl, turn and toss high like an acrobat in the circus.

Catherine beamed as the operator buckled her into the harness and began to lift her cable. We all watched as she was elevated and then released to bounce off the trampoline, gradually bouncing higher and higher. We laughed as she squealed through somersaults and tricks in the air.

Sophia could hardly contain herself. She hopped and begged us to let her try. She was thrilled when, by standing on her very tiptoes, she barely made the height requirement.

Confident and full of anticipation, Sophia sat down in the harness and the ride operator strapped her in, checking the buckle to make sure it was secure. Then he flipped the switch to elevate her. For the first time, Sophia looked down at her toes—

then at the ground, which was getting smaller and smaller in her view as she rose into the air. With each inch upward, alone in that seat, my little girl's confidence oozed visibly out of her. She froze—and then her bottom lip trembled and her face began to melt into a frown. I knew what was coming.

Though she was well above my head, I could see the tears welling in her eyes. Then she could control them no longer. As the dam of tears burst, she wailed in fear.

I jumped over the barrier and stood directly under her, beside the trampoline. "Sophia!" I shouted up. "Look into Mummy's eyes. Don't take your eyes off Mummy, and you are going to be okay. You can do this! You are a big girl. You will love this!"

Sophia looked right at me, and there was an instant change in her countenance when she saw my smile. She relaxed and even started to smile herself as the safety seat took her higher.

"You're going to bounce now," I said. "It'll be fun. Here it comes!"

The operator released the cable, and she bounced, and bounced again, still watching me, her smile wider now.

"Can you turn?" I said. "Can you twirl?"

She tried, and then jumped higher, and now she was laughing. Within a couple of bounces, she was jumping higher than her big sister—because she was no longer afraid. She was taking huge risks and delighting in where they took her. She knew I was right there with her, and would hang onto her in spirit to the very end, and in the meantime she was free and soaring like she couldn't even have imagined moments before.

This is such a wonderful picture of how God works in us: confront a fear and take a risk. He's there with us, before, during, and after.

He promises to be our light in the darkness and our strength (Psalm 21:1; 27:1).

He reminds us not to be dismayed, because he will help us and hold us (Isaiah 41:10).

He tells us to be of good courage because he will never leave nor forsake us (Deuteronomy 31:6).

He exhorts us to be strong and courageous (Joshua 1:6).

He delivers us from our troubles and doubts and fears so that we may taste and see his goodness (Psalm 34).

So that we might taste and see.

God's power is *not* invisible. It's real. It's an undeniable force, and it lives in us. As we fix our eyes on him, we see his love, we taste his power, and it feeds us. It helps us grow stronger—so strong, in fact, that like Sophia we find every bit of strength we need to soar above and beyond any fear holding us back.

When we keep our eyes on him, he takes us out of the constraints that otherwise bind us in fear. We are no longer restricted and trapped. We are free. Our world and our lives are enlarged, and the possibilities for the miraculous are increased. We achieve the impossible by focusing on the God with whom all things are possible. We are enabled to reach and rescue the people who have fallen through society's cracks. We rescue slaves who otherwise would be captive still. We help the defeated who otherwise would languish. We find the lost. We bring healing to the damaged and diseased. We open the eyes of the blind. We go places we never imagined without sinking or being swallowed by our own fears.

MAKING THE STORM INTO A PLAYGROUND

To our oldest daughter Catherine, then five, the storm came upon us like a monster out of nowhere. She had begun our lengthy road trip home by immediately falling asleep with sunlight streaming through the car windows. After sleeping through much of the journey, she woke to see the weather's fury unleashed outside.

Gray skies darkened, and a hard rain turned into a hailstorm just as we pulled into our driveway. Nick grabbed our bags as I grabbed the girls, racing everything and everyone inside. We'd barely made it indoors when the storm reached new and frightening heights, and behind us hail pounded and pummeled the car, denting the hood and roof. Windows cracked, and we could see windows of cars and houses up and down the street breaking. Roof tiles on the houses began to shatter and fall to the ground. Water splashed violently out of backyard pools and over fences. Thunder punctuated the incessant pounding of hail. A tree, struck by a lightning bolt and gale-force winds, splintered and fell through the roof of the house behind us; still another fell across our neighbor's driveway.

Sophia, our baby, slept through it all. But, terrified, Catherine began to scream and cry. Even after the hail stopped, Catherine would not be comforted. She cried and shrieked until finally, exhausted, she fell into a fitful sleep.

I expected that she would wake at peace, and the fear inside her would have passed like the hail outside. I was wrong.

She rose the next morning asking if it was going to rain and hail again. She worriedly checked outside through the window all day, trying to gauge the weather. For days following, she would ask Nick and me, sometimes as many as five times in a morning or afternoon, if it was going to rain. Every time we needed to take the car anywhere, she obsessed over the weather. If it started to rain while we were in the car, she would cry. If we were home when the rain began, she would run into her room and pull the curtains. She would not play outside with her friends if there was even a hint of gray sky.

Catherine's fear of storms was so strong that she was willing to change everything else in her life to avoid them.

I knew I had to intervene. She couldn't live her life in fear of rain, because one thing we can be sure of about the future is that rain will come. There will be storms. Hiding from them or trying to avoid them won't stop them. Catherine could shut herself away from the storms only by shutting herself away from life.

The irony was not lost on me—I had spent much of my life shutting myself off from fully experiencing life because of my fear of flying! But avoiding my fears had not immunized me from danger—it came anyway, even while we were unpacking our car and making our way into the house. Danger comes, no matter how much we try to keep it at bay. Trying to live a safe, controlled life does not stop danger. You can't run from fear, because fear will catch up with you. The only thing to do is face fear head-on, lest the root of fear become a full-grown weed that can take over your life. Instead, we can dispel fear with God's presence.

Catherine wouldn't have gone along willingly with an intervention, but then who does? I knew that my daughter feared storms so much she was willing to forsake many things she loved—opportunities for fun, friends, and activities. If she didn't conquer her fear of a little rain, she would be overwhelmed by even lesser storms as she—and her fear—grew. She could be paralyzed by fear.

So we didn't talk about this. The next rainy day that came, I grabbed Catherine and took her outside. At first she cried, but I insisted on making a game of the rain. I began to jump and stomp in the puddles. I laughed at the sky. I rejoiced in the rain. And surprised by my thrill, my absence of fear, Catherine stopped crying and began to laugh. Soon she was on the ground, stomping in the puddles with me.

Now I can't keep Catherine inside when it rains. She grabs her sister and they put on their gumboots to run into the puddles and splash.

The very thing Catherine once feared has become her playground.

EMBOLDENED TO GO WHERE YOU NEVER IMAGINED

In Matthew 14:22–33, when a storm came upon Peter, a fisherman used to choppy waters, he faced the choice of giving in to fear or stepping out in faith. Peter knew how to make his way through a storm. He practically lived on the water! But he also knew his limitations. All his fears were whispering in his head, as they were in the heads of his companions: *The winds are too fierce, the waves too high, the boat too fragile in this gale.* Everyone in the boat began to cower in fear, their concentration fixed on all the dangers of the storm.

Just as Peter was about to give up himself, he looked out on the water and saw . . .

Jesus?

Yes, Jesus. Walking on the water, walking through the storm! He called to Peter to step out into the storm as well, to step out of the boat and onto the water, to step into the danger and out of fear, to take a step of faith.

And Peter wanted to do it!

"Come," Jesus said to him (Matthew 14:29).

So, believing that with Jesus, one can do anything, Peter took that step of faith, his eyes fixed on the Lord. One step— and just like that, he was walking through the storm, undaunted by danger, defying it even, doing the miraculous.

And then an especially large gust of wind swept over Peter, spray whipped his face, and his attention was back on the storm. *The waves are too high*, he must have thought, *the wind too fierce, Jesus too far away* . . .

But Peter's vision was clouded by the storm. His sight was deceiving him. Jesus was never far away. He was with Peter in the storm, right there when the greatest gale blew.

"Immediately," the Bible says, "Jesus reached out his hand and caught [Peter] (Matthew 14:31). " 'You of little faith,' he said, 'why did you doubt?' "

Why *do* we doubt?

Jesus beckons us to come. If we stay focused on him, we will be able to go anywhere and do whatever is required of us. If we take our eyes off him and stare at the storm, at the danger, we will surely sink. We will never go to the millions trapped out there in the darkness of human trafficking, or the millions without water, or the millions suffering abuse, disease, famine, injustice, loneliness, or hopelessness.

To get to them, we may have to walk on water.

Fear and faith cannot coexist. As I faced my own limitations and fears, was I going to believe God's truth or the lies of the enemy, reflected in my own emotions? Was I going to choose fear of the world — or faith in the one who has overcome the world?

Choose to trust the Creator of the universe, the one who hung the moon and placed the stars and fixed the sky.

"Go," he says . . .

". . . and make disciples of all nations, baptizing them in the name of the Father and of the Son and of the Holy Spirit, and teaching them to obey everything I have commanded you."

And then he gives the promise that makes it all possible — that makes it possible, too, for us to live undaunted: "And surely I am with you always, to the very end of the age" (Matthew 28:19–20).

He doesn't ask us to go *as long as* or *if* or *after* he removes all danger and takes away all fear. He asks us to go *in spite of* and *even if* and *anyway*. He says simply: *Believe. Go with me.*

He's been saying this all my life, giving me the courage to look fear in the face and dare to go where he is calling me to go.

When I wanted to go to Bible college but feared I'd get booted out once the professors discovered how little I really knew, Jesus asked, *Will you go with me?*

"Yes, Lord," I told him. "I'll go anyway, because I want to better know and understand your Word and pass on the good news."

When I was afraid to marry because my trust had been broken, and I was riddled with scar tissue, he asked: *But, Chris, will you go with me?*

"Yes, Lord," I said. "I'll go — even though I'm afraid of being hurt again and I'm damaged by being hurt before — because

I don't want to miss out on the relationships you ordained for me or the love that's waiting for me."

When God began to open doors for me to talk to teenagers in high school, I was terrified. *What if they ridicule and heckle me or simply refuse to listen?* But Jesus asked simply, *Will you go with me?*

"Yes, Lord. I'll go even though they might not listen to me — because what if just one life is touched and transformed? It will be worth it for that one.

And when he brought me opportunities to share about him around the world — and to get there not on a slow boat, but on one of the jet planes that terrified me — he asked once more, *Will you go with me?*

And as in every other thing he had asked me to do, I knew that I did indeed have a choice. Jesus always gives us this choice. I could choose to allow my fears to rule me. Or I could believe that the God who made the heavens and had called me to this task was unstoppable, and unafraid of the gravity he had created. If he wanted me to cross the globe to be his hands and feet in getting to one of the lost and lonely, to someone broken in a ditch and waiting for a Samaritan, then he could uphold a plane in the sky.

UNDAUNTED, YOU REACH YOUR DESTINY

That power, the power of Jesus' presence, is what kept me calm in my seat on that flight from Chicago to North Carolina, where, with a malfunctioning landing gear, we were in danger of crashing upon landing. As the captain announced our approach back at O'Hare Airport and instructed us in how to prepare, I watched the people around me brace themselves for the worst. They held onto the armrests of their seats, or the hand or arm of the person sitting next to them. Many audibly prayed.

I closed my eyes.

My hand in Nick's, I prayed quietly, silently: *Lord, I am ever so grateful you did not let me succumb to my fear of flying, but rather helped me choose to push through that fear. There were times I never thought I would or could get back on a plane, but I so wanted your will and purpose for my life. How many times have I had to choose to get on a flight afraid—and yet every time, you have been with me, comforting me, enabling me, strengthening me. And because of that I have been able to go to so many cities and nations around the world, and reach people I would never have otherwise been able to reach.* I thought of God's promise in 2 Timothy 1:7. *Lord*, I prayed, *like every other time, I choose to remind myself that you have not given us a spirit of fear, but of power and of love and of a sound mind.*

I heard and felt rubber hitting the tarmac. All of the passengers erupted in spontaneous applause. As we gradually decelerated down the long runway, we passed awaiting police cars with sirens blasting, as well as fire trucks, ambulances, and ground personnel.

Yet we landed without incident, and within minutes the door of the plane was opening. Light streamed in.

Once I feared flying with a paralyzing fear that kept me bound to the island of Australia. But because Jesus calmed my fears, as he did with Peter in the storm while walking on the water, the very thing I once feared has become my vehicle to minister to others in darkness, to go and do likewise.

We live in a dark world. Rain falls. Storms come. Lightning strikes. Your life can shatter. The roof can fall in. You can be damaged. As long as you live, you will have something to lose—little pieces of yourself. The people you love, the life choices you cherish—there is always something at risk, something dear. Some cause for fear. We can choose to surrender to that fear and let it rule our lives, or we can surrender to Christ all of those things we love and fear to lose, and then live fearlessly—undaunted.

Some people have paid a horror of a price to live in fear. All they see is the darkness. All they have to clutch is their fear or their despair, their loneliness, their despondency.

But those who follow Christ have the light. We know his love. We have hope. We can bring the news of his grace, of change.

Do you love me? Jesus asks.

Undaunted, we can answer *yes*—and prepare to serve him without fear.

chapter 7

I Once Was Lost

Remember that day in Thessaloniki, when Sonia turned to me and said, "Why didn't you come sooner"? The urgency in her question was visceral, desperate, undeniable—and yet that urgency may be hard for many people around the world to understand. We aren't being attacked or degraded or enslaved. We're not hungry. We're not thirsty. We have comfortable, warm clothes to wear and a roof over our heads. We're safe.

When you're not lost—when you're safe—it's hard to understand the urgency of needing to be found, needing to be rescued.

And yet all of us who are believers in Christ have a way of understanding that urgency. "Lost" is what all of us once were, apart from Christ—before he found us and adopted us into his family. Even so, maybe you were saved as a child, or maybe the decision was more an intellectual one than an emotional one for you. And maybe we live lives so insulated from desperate, urgent need that we simply can't understand Sonia's level of desperation on any level.

Occasionally, though, God sends us a reminder . . .

EXPLORING THE DAINTREE RAINFOREST —
CLOSE UP

Our Jeep—driven by Mick and now definitely out of control—lurched and fishtailed down the steep, muddy track of the mountainside. The curve in the primitive road was approaching much too fast, and the brakes weren't responding on the mud. I gritted my teeth and closed my eyes—we were about to go off the side of the road. Would we roll? Was this it?

Mick cut the wheel and tried to stay on the road, but it was no use—off the side we went. The jeep nosedived, and we crashed through the underbrush, bouncing crazily as those of us inside crashed off the jeep's roof and sides and each other. At the mercy of gravity and physics, we slid faster and faster, more and more out of control, until we reached the bottom and slammed into a huge, muddy ditch.

We were stuck in a bog like an almond in a chocolate bar.

The five of us—my friends Kylie, Sally, Mick, Paul, and I—were on the last day of our summer trip and had decided to drive through the Daintree Rainforest, one of Australia's natural wonders and among the oldest preserved ecosystems in the world. Using an old, faded map we'd found discarded at a diner, we'd chosen what looked like an interesting route and set out. We'd had a wonderful and scenic drive up to this point—eucalyptus and red gum trees so large our group of five could not encircle one vine-covered trunk by clasping hands around it. Miles of orchids, ferns, and wild ginger stretched beneath palms whose giant green branches brushed you like fans as you walked past. Cascading waterfalls with misty sprays would cool you in the tropic heat.

It had been great fun. Until now.

"I couldn't stop!" Mick gasped. "Everybody okay?"

Slowly, we each checked ourselves and responded, "Yeah." I pried my fingers off the seat back in front of me, where I'd grabbed on for dear life. Each of us was stunned and shaken.

Oh well, I decided, rubbing my neck, *there's nothing more to say or do but get out of the Jeep and start pushing it from the mud.*

I remember the slurp and the ooze around my legs as I stepped into the swale. *Yuck,* I thought. *I wonder what else is in here.* I was still up for an adventure, but this wasn't quite what I'd had in mind.

JUST A WALK IN THE WOODS

For two hours, Kylie, Sally, Mick, Paul, and I pushed, shoved, lifted, and waded through the mud to dislodge our tiny, Tonka-like vehicle. Finally it sat on reasonably level and dry ground, and it looked as if, with our four-wheel drive, we'd be able to make it back to the road at the bottom of the hill up ahead. Tired and covered in brown slime, we rested a minute against the Jeep's side.

Then Mick jumped into the driver's seat to start up the engine for our ride back. He turned the key and after a momentary sputter ... nothing. He turned the key again. Sputter, sputter. Nothing. At first we thought maybe mud had clogged the fuel line. Then Paul pointed to the gas gauge flashing red. We'd been having so much fun that none of us had noticed that we'd used up the gas in the main tank and were running on the reserve. The slide must have burned the last of our fuel.

"Well," I said, laughing. "Looks like we're walkin'."

"Yeah," Kylie said. "But surely, given the amount of time we've driven, we can't be that far from the end of this road."

"There ought to be someplace ahead where we can call for help."

Though none of us had a cell phone, our spirits were high.

"This is going to make one great story," I said, eyebrows raised, grinning.

We started down the road, laughing and playing, not particularly worried.

Before long, though, we started to get more anxious to reach somewhere that looked more like civilization. We seemed to be going deeper *into* the rainforest, rather than coming out. I realized how thirsty I was, and, come to think of it, hungry too. My feet began to hurt. Flip-flops weren't the best footwear for walking through a dense rainforest. And the sunlight, already dim under the canopy of trees, was beginning to fade. Cool breezes filtered through the wet foliage from the coast. After being so hot earlier, now I felt chilled in my thin T-shirt and shorts.

We walked on, still merry, but our laughter subdued a notch as we each entertained the same wish: *Shower. Something to eat. Something to drink.* Silently, I prayed we'd find our way out of the woods sooner rather than later. I wasn't scared—I just wanted to get back to the fun of our wooded wonderland adventure. I felt sure we weren't far from a place to grab dinner (or at least a snack), fuel for the Jeep, and maybe even a lift back to it so we could be on our way. I figured no one would put a road to nowhere in the depths of the rainforest. There must be some civilization at the other end.

And then the sun began to set.

NIGHT IN THE WILD

Sunset alerted us to our perfect storm of danger: The trail seemed to take us only deeper into the dark rainforest, not a hotel or beam of light in any direction. The dense green foliage covering and connecting the trees was now almost black.

Suddenly it occurred to me that no one knew where we were. Our decision to explore the Daintree had been a spur-of-the-moment thing, discussed only among ourselves. And frankly, we didn't even know our location in this twelve hundred-kilometer-square piece of wild. Even if we did, I had no ability to read the map and wasn't so sure I could trust my friends' directional skills. In the fading light, we soon wouldn't be able to make out the road ahead.

When you're in such a predicament, suddenly you begin to

hear things you hadn't before: the shuffling of creatures over-head and underfoot, the whoosh and brush of branches.

I began to hear running water. We had come to a river, and there was no way forward but through it.

We stood at the bank a moment, hesitating. I think the same thought crossed each of our minds: *Are we really going to try crossing a river? Shouldn't we turn back? But we've come so far already. Surely we aren't far from some help . . .*

Mick, who carried the video camera we'd brought to record our adventures, announced we had about thirty minutes of bat-tery life left—significant not because we needed video footage to document our stupidity, but because the camera's floodlight was our only source of light.

Thirty minutes? We'd been walking for hours. Thirty minutes wouldn't be nearly enough time. The dark was falling fast—al-ready it was so dim that I couldn't see entirely across the river.

We looked to one another and nodded. Now, we decided, would be a good time to turn on the camera—we needed light to guide us across the river.

Mick flipped on the switch.

The beams cutting through the dark illuminated our prog-ress. In every direction, as far as we could see, were towering trees covered in vines and wild plants. Silhouetted in the back-ground were mountain peaks reaching into a fathomless sky of distant stars.

We looked at each other, then quickly away again. It was al-most unbearable to admit, to see the recognition in each other's eyes.

We were lost.

HELPLESS AND HOPELESS

It was only when the light illuminated the darkness that I real-ized the seriousness of our situation and just how hopelessly lost we were.

The facts were plain. We'd plunged deep into the wild of the Daintree. It was night, and we were on foot with poor shoes, without food or water, protective clothing, a guidebook on surviving in the rainforest, a cell phone, or even a clue on how to get back to civilization. *How foolish we've been*, I thought. No one was looking for us. And even when we turned up missing, no one would have any idea where to look. We were novices, tourists out for a fun summer vacation ride, city people with no idea of what we'd just exposed ourselves to — and we were in one of the oldest rainforests in the world, home to venomous snakes, lizards, and spiders. Even without those odds, my idea of camping was more like slow room service than sleeping in a tent or under stars on the mossy ground at the base of a tree.

Just a day earlier, that would have been a joke. We weren't laughing now. It's not that we were terrified. We probably should have been *more* terrified than we were. But we did realize that we needed help. We'd gotten ourselves into a terrible situation and none of us knew how we were going to get out.

With the battery burning, we braced ourselves to cross the river.

Silently, we stepped, single file, into the water. The river was shallow enough at this spot that we could cross by walking, but I almost yelped because it was so freezing. Instead, I focused on getting across. The boys helped Kylie, Sally, and me as we struggled for footing in our flip-flops. I wanted to freak out — the camera's stark light revealed cockroaches on the banks — but kept praying my way across.

As if on cue, just as we all reached the far bank, the light of the video camera went out.

How eerie and yet comforting at the same time, I thought. "Thank you, God," I prayed. "You saw us through. Now see us safely home." Though we had no idea what was ahead, God had seen us through what I was sure would be the worst of our wandering.

We had a little moonlight to guide us. Silent now, we walked through the fringes of vines and branches. We began to hear little pings and patters. *Rain.* The scent of the storm, which might have seemed pleasantly fragrant earlier, came on strong and signaled more trouble. I looked at my watch as the downpour set in: one in the morning. It had been twelve hours since lunch. I was beginning to feel the effects of dehydration. My mouth felt dry, like I'd been chewing cotton balls, but my stomach was angry, growling for food, and the rest of my body was chilled. The rain added more than discomfort. In my shorts and T-shirt, I shivered. I was slightly lightheaded and finding it difficult to focus. I no longer wondered if we'd get back in time to catch our flight home. I began to wonder how we would get back at all.

"We've got to stop," Sally said. She looked as sick as I felt.

It was too dark to proceed anyway. We looked for some shelter where we could rest until dawn. Though there were trees everywhere—this was the rainforest!—none seemed to offer a ceiling from the storm. We hunted for fallen branches and loose sticks to fashion into a makeshift shelter. We finally huddled together under our excuse for a lean-to against a massive tree, our only refuge. I rubbed my hands and feet. Prickly vines and spiny bushes and vegetation had cut and bruised my tired limbs. I felt dirty, fatigued, hungry, thirsty—and hopeless. We were silent, undoubtedly all thinking the same thing: that none of us knew how to get out of this mess.

Exhausted, we dozed, often jerking awake with pain or cold. None of us really slept. We nodded deeply into our own thoughts, mostly of our loved ones back home, knowing they had no idea that we were lost in the rainforest instead of asleep in our hotel beds and packed for tomorrow's flight home. *Not one other human being on earth knows our trouble,* I thought. *But you know, God. Could you somehow rescue us from this mess we've gotten ourselves into? I'm sorry we were so irresponsible. I know this is no one's fault but our own. We have no one to blame but ourselves. We've been unwise, and this is our consequence. But help us, God. Please, please help us.*

Five miserable hours later, the sun came up. Once again, the light showed us how desperate our situation was. We were filthy and mud-caked, and our eyes were bloodshot and dark-rimmed with exhaustion. Though the rain had stopped, we were soaked and aching. Sally and Paul couldn't even walk, they had cut their feet so badly gathering sticks and branches before we'd climbed under the tree. I felt the sting of every one of my own cuts on my legs, hands, and feet.

For another hour, we sat nursing ourselves, evaluating every possible course of action. Keep walking forward? We had no idea what was ahead, and we were feeling weaker rather than stronger. Wait where we were? We could be waiting here for weeks. No one was looking for us, and what were the chances of someone venturing along? Maybe we should try to go back—but then we'd come so far. Going back would take at least another day, maybe two considering our deteriorating physical state. Every option seemed a dead end.

"Enough," Mick said finally. "I'm making an executive decision. I feel strong. I'm going ahead for help. The rest of you should wait here—you'd only slow me down anyway. I'll send help back for you."

Though none of us said it, the rest were undoubtedly thinking what I was: *not likely*. Even so, Mick was right—we had to do something. If we all just sat here, we would inevitably die. Feeling grim and scared, we reluctantly agreed. But first, we decided, the rest of us should move to higher ground. There was a cliff nearby; we would perch on its edge.

"The chances of you finding us again are better that way," Paul told Mick, "if you're successful ..."

That *if* echoed in all our minds.

From our new, higher vantage point, Paul, Kylie, Sally, and I watched him retreat into the forest, and then fell into silence, again drifting into our own thoughts.

I sat on the wet ground, pulling my knees up to my chin and hugging my legs. The pressure of limb against limb eased slightly the sting of my cuts. But my bruises from the slide in the car and our push through the underbrush began to ache all over again.

Over the next five hours, we each fidgeted every time a branch twitched or bush crackled in the forest. At ten that morning, I thought of our plane taking off to return to Sydney. The flight was three hours, and only when we didn't disembark would anyone even think to try to contact us. They would trace us to the hotel, where we had not yet checked out, but no one would know where we had gone. They wouldn't know where to even begin to look. How would they find us in this wild, dense rainforest? Our Jeep was as lost to the world as we were, hidden deep in the forest, slid off the road. Surely the night's rains had washed away even the evidence of our slide as well as any of our footprints.

Another four hours passed. My stomach ached for food, and though it was the middle of the day, I was shivering. The elements and our exposure were taking their toll. I worried about Mick. What if he hurt himself? Or encountered some dangerous animal? My mind was having trouble focusing, and I slipped into despair. It would take a miracle to get us out of this situation. Things would only get worse: the hunger, the hurt.

I began to give up hope of rescue.

Slowly, hurting with each step, I gathered some palm and fern leaves to make myself a deathbed. I spread them out and lay carefully upon them, eyes closed, arms folded across my chest.

"What are you doing?" Paul asked.

"If we're found, I want to look peaceful," I said.

"Chris, you are such a drama queen," Kylie said.

I knew she was right, but I also believed that this probably was the very end. I had always wondered how I would feel when this moment came, and I was somewhat surprised at how calm I felt. I thought about my family and all my relationships and life up to this point. "God," I prayed, "I am so grateful for the fact that you saved me and allowed me to serve you, but I really didn't think I would come home like this. I thought you had so much more for me. At least I know I really do believe in you, Lord, and I'm ready to meet you face-to-face. Please be with my mum and family and team as they deal with this. Lord, I am so sorry we were so careless. I know we should have been more careful, but I can't change that now."

Kylie jolted me. "Do you hear that?" she whispered, breathless.

"What?" Paul asked.

I listened.

"Don't you hear?" she insisted.

All I heard was Kylie rustling, trying to stand. *She's delirious*, I thought. *How nice, God, for you to give her a hallucination to get her through the passing from this life to the next.*

Then I felt a slight vibration, a tremor in the trees, on the ground, followed by the sound of a steady, beating whir. I rubbed my ears. The sound didn't go away. In fact, it was getting louder. I felt a force of air and opened one eye.

THE DIFFERENCE A DAY MAKES

Kylie and Paul were standing, waving madly at the sky, shouting, "Here! We're here!" Their shouts and an even stronger rush of air made me sit up and look around to see—a helicopter. Mick leaned out from the side of it as it hovered just above us. He too waved, beaming.

I jumped up and ran to the cliff's edge. I will never forget standing there on that precipice, yelling, "We're saved! We're saved! We're saved!" Overjoyed and relieved and incredulously happy, I wanted to hop up and down. Instead, I froze.

It wasn't just the sharp drop over the cliff's edge or my sore feet and aching limbs that stopped me. It was the words. As clearly as I have ever heard the voice of God, I heard him that day: *Yes, Christine, you are saved. Remember what it is to be saved. Remember what it was to be lost. Remember the darkness and the difference between feeling carefree one morning and by evening sad and scared and sorry for being careless. Remember that I am here. Remember that I want to save every soul. And remember what it is to be unable on your own ability to get out of the dark.*

A ladder dropped down from the sky. I blinked up into what was startling light after our dark night and day of the soul. As I grabbed onto the first rung, it was like grabbing God's hand, and it filled me with gratitude. In the light of day, with hope, I thought: *I will never forget.* How could I? A minute ago I was utterly hopeless, preparing to die, feeling forgotten and far from help, beyond the reach of any rescue, in such a strange and unforgiving place, surrounded by predators, aching and cut, sore and soaked by rain, fear, and despair.

The rescue team dropped down a safety cable, and I wrapped it around my waist. I climbed up the ladder rungs, dangling there above the wild where moments ago I'd expected to die. How different the rainforest looked in the light of hope. *Just trees*, I thought. Above, the rescue team was reaching to pull me safely into the helicopter. Once inside, I marveled at the change made by the hand reached out to rescue. I even laughed, because I couldn't help but think that this seemed more like a scene in some TV rescue series than an actual experience in my own life.

I looked around me at my friends, now safe in this expensive helicopter. The rescue team had dropped everything to look for us, find us, and bring us out of the dark and danger. I realized: *Saving costs something. Rescuing risks everything.* That is exactly what God has done for us by sending Jesus into the world to seek and save that which was lost.

As I undid the safety harness, I looked up to heaven and whispered, "God, I will not forget those still lost in the darkness."

I REMEMBER

I told God that I would not forget, and I haven't. I remember that feeling of exhilaration and relief when I saw the helicopter and realized that we were saved. And I remember God's words: *"Remember what it is to be saved. Remember what it was to be lost."* I have remembered many times since then. Just as I remembered that day in Thessaloniki when Sonia asked, "Why didn't you come sooner?"

I could understand her desperation, her sense of urgency, because I remembered my own.

For the desperate, the hungry, the oppressed, for those in pain, no rescue can come soon enough. And when the lost call to us for rescue, God doesn't command us to be supermen. He commands us to be willing. He'll do the rest.

Something I already knew from the Bible was now true to me in a new way: There are so many who have no way out, unless we go to rescue them. The words of the prophets took on new meaning. I said them silently to God, a vow that came from the place of knowing what it meant to be rescued: *Here I am, Lord. Send me!* (Isaiah 6:8)

If we make that promise to God — *Send me* — what changes are we committing to?

"Send Me" Means Reaching Out to the Lost

It's so natural, after being rescued, to simply go back to your life, to business-as-usual. After a harrowing experience, you're yearning for normalcy. You want to—and sometimes do—forget that hopeless, horrifying moment of being forgotten in darkness. Going back there to warn others is hard work—and trying to rescue others in those perilous places sounds risky.

That, I believe, is why Jesus told story after story about how easy it is to be lost—and how remarkable it is to be saved. Stories of people hopeless and hurting. People who need living water, people whose souls are tattered, with the dark closing in around them and time running out.

In Luke's gospel, chapter 15, he tells of a lost sheep—and then, as if he sensed we'd miss the message, he tells of a lost coin, and then of a lost son.

These stories, he says, will remind you of something I want you always to remember: *No matter how deep the pit or dark the night, I will always look for you and rescue you because I love you with an everlasting love. You are precious to me. Even when you mess up, even when you're careless or mistaken or afraid or broken or weak, I still love you. Even when you are incapable of doing anything for anyone, including yourself, I still love you. And just as I come for you, I come for all those who have made mistakes, and those who are overlooked, for those devalued and despised. I come for all the wrong people—the careless and uncared for, the merry and miserable. I come for the lost, whether the lost is a silly sheep, a silver coin, or a squandering son.*

"Send Me" Means Looking for the Lost, Even If It Is Only One Person

If you have one hundred sheep and one wanders off, Jesus tells us, that's the one you go after to rescue. Isn't the one as valuable as each of the ninety-nine?

In natural disasters and in time of war, medical personnel often perform something they call *triage*. It means that they examine the injured and determine which have the best chance of living. They concentrate their efforts on those they think they can save—and, with regret, allow the others to die, or perhaps to rally and recover on their own.

Jesus doesn't do triage. He leaves the healthy ninety-nine safe in their pen while he goes out into the night looking for the one who's lost, sick, depressed, disappointed, wounded, enslaved. And when he has found it, he lays it across his shoulders and in celebration calls together his neighbors, saying, "Rejoice with me; I have found my lost sheep" (Luke 15:6).

How could an almighty God do any less? Can you imagine what his message to us would be otherwise? "I'll come after you and save you—*if* I'm not too busy saving others, and *if* my attention isn't needed keeping the ninety-nine others safe. After all, you probably got into this mess yourself, and it wouldn't be fair to deprive the others, who are being good, of my time and attention just to keep coming after you. I'll help you if circumstances allow. Otherwise, you're on your own."

Never in Scripture does Jesus give a message anything like this. Instead, he promises to come after the one, because each one is precious to him. Each one.

"Send Me" Means Seeking the Lost — Even If We Fear Them

It's true — many of us *fear* the lost, and because of that, we're reluctant to go out into the world to seek them.

Why would we fear the lost? Many reasons. Maybe because, often, they're so needy and desperate. We're afraid that they will attach themselves to us, leech-like, and beg for one thing after another: our time, our money, our emotional support, a place in our home ("just until I get back on my feet"), a ride to work — and on and on.

Maybe we fear them because they are so "other" than us. A different lifestyle, different life choices, different language and clothing styles and foods and music and sense of humor. Will they accept us? Will they laugh at us behind our backs? Will they despise us even as we sacrifice for them? Are they, perhaps, even a danger to us? Might they be willing to take by force those things we don't offer freely? Will we feel uncomfortable, uneasy, in their midst?

When Jesus urged Peter to feed his sheep, he didn't offer a list of excuses he would accept. "Feed my sheep — unless it becomes inconvenient or the sheep become too demanding. Feed my sheep — unless you're afraid of the big ram who protects the flock. Feed my sheep — unless you're afraid that they'll charge you, snatch the food out of your hand, and trample you."

He just asked Peter to feed his sheep.

"Send Me" Means Seeking the Lost — No Matter How They Got Lost

In the story of the lost coin, the coin didn't lose itself. A woman who had ten silver coins lost one. Was she so busy she forgot where she'd placed it? Did she take her eyes off her treasure for only a moment—and a thief snatched it? Did she trip, spilling all her coins onto the floor, where one rolled out of sight? Did an addiction cause her to gamble away a part of her money—and then even more, in a desperate attempt to win it back?

Some people are lost not because of something they willfully did, but because of a place they fell into, or because of circumstance. They are lost because of the words of an insensitive teacher, the neglect of an absent parent, the malice of an abuser. Maybe they've been abducted by a trafficker who sees them not as persons but as commodities to be bought and sold to the highest bidder. Maybe a corrupt ruler has mismanaged all of their country's resources, leaving the innocent poor with no food, no water, no health care or education or basic human services. In any case, the lost are people who have lost their purpose, their potential, perhaps even their destiny.

Maybe *the one* is a single mom whose income pays only some of the bills and is maxing out her credit cards to cover the rest of her family's necessities. Or maybe *the one* is the couple working so hard at their jobs and managing their home that they're drifting apart, and the intimacy of their marriage has been lost. Or maybe *the one* is the CEO who has worked his way to the top of the corporate ladder—but is experiencing such dissatisfaction and malaise that he's wondering whether that top rung is actually up against the right wall.

The one may be someone who has lived a life of crime that has landed him in jail. *The one* may be someone who has willfully hurt another. *The one* may be selfish, addicted, immoral, arrogant, a mocker, a scoffer, a murderer, or a prostitute. If our example is Jesus, who stood up for the woman caught in adultery and the greedy, dishonest tax collector and the thief on the cross, then we won't distinguish between the one who is lost because of circumstances beyond his control and the one who willfully and willingly put himself there.

The third "lost" story Jesus tells is a famous one—about a son who has been given everything, not only his father's resources, but his heart and blessing, and then squanders it all and descends into humiliation and poverty. The father is willing to overlook his son's transgressions because he's so glad to have back the son he loves so much.

Let's face it: Many of us secretly feel—as did the older brother in the story—that the younger son had made his own deathbed, and he ought to sleep in it.

No, Jesus says. The squandering son is as important and beloved as the dutiful older brother, or the little lost lamb too preoccupied with lunch to keep up with the flock, or the money misplaced by circumstance. Why do we sometimes feel that the seriously, deeply lost should be on their own—that they got themselves into this mess of their own volition and should get themselves out or stay that way? Can you imagine if the rescue squad sent for my friends and me had said: "Sorry, no can do. We can't rescue those who get lost because of their own stupidity. Those people can just die and face the consequences of their actions."

No. When someone is trapped in a burning building, you don't try to work out what caused the fire and then decide whether the people inside get your sympathy. When people are in danger of burning up, you rush to save them. Especially if you remember how much it hurts to be burned.

No matter how the treasure of a soul comes to be lost, our job is to go and rescue and save what is precious.

Were you blameless when Jesus came for you?

Jesus says that even God calls the angels together to rejoice over the precious soul that's been found (Luke 15:7, 10). We were made from the dust of the earth—and yet even the humblest and least deserving of us are of such value to heaven!

THE LOVE OF GOD IS DEEPER STILL

You understand Christ's deep desire to find and rescue *the one* when the one who's lost is someone you love.

I was in a London bookstore on Oxford Street, one of the busiest streets in the world, when I lost my precious one. I'd looked away from my little girl for just a moment, and when I turned back around, Catherine, three years old at the time, was gone. Vanished! I looked out at the teeming sidewalk of people, first confused, then frantic. She was so small, and the crowd so big! I ran outside in search of her. I didn't care how I looked, how I sounded, what people thought—I just wanted to find my girl. I climbed on top of a mailbox, screaming at the top of my lungs: "Catherine! Catherine!" I stopped strangers, demanding: "Have you seen my daughter? Have you seen a tiny three-year-old girl? *Have you?*"

I would have kept it up—and even gotten louder and more obnoxious—until I found Catherine.

And then I saw her. She had just walked around the corner to the children's book section and was sitting behind a bookshelf, mostly hidden. While I had been frantic, she had been reading, happily oblivious to my anxiety.

I will never forget that feeling of panic. *My child is lost! Where could she be? Does someone have her? Is she in harm's way? What's happening to her? Is she frightened? Is she calling for me? Does she know I'm looking for her?* There was nothing I would not have done, if in fact she had been lost or taken, to rescue her! I was desperate. I wanted my child. There were thousands of people around, but I was desperate to find just one—my daughter.

Maybe you've experienced something similar yourself. It's the most horrifying feeling. You feel physically ill. Your adrenalin starts going into overdrive, your mind races out of control, imagining every possible worst scenario. Your heart beats so violently you think it will pop out of your chest. You feel hopeless and helpless and crazy to find your one.

Magnify that feeling times a thousand, times ten thousand. God loves each one of us, each child and each parent and each cop and each bureaucrat and each drug dealer and each retail clerk and each athlete and each murderer, that much more than we love our children, even our spouses. And his drive to save each of us is far stronger than my drive, that day, to find and rescue my daughter.

God's heart beats for every lost person every single second of every single day. He misses the lost. The world is such a dark place, dense and full of danger. The warning signs are not always clear or noticed. There are so many who need rescuers, so many who need others to help their wandering ways, so many who are simply foolish, careless sheep. Each of them is God's missing treasure, his beloved though willful and prodigal child.

There are so many like we, too, were once.

That's what he wants us to remember. We, too, once were lost and now are found. And because we've been found, we are part of his search-and-rescue team. The light we craved once, the light he brought to us to illuminate our own rescue, is what he sends us back into the dark to carry.

"You are the light of the world," he says (Matthew 5:14). *You have what it takes to bring home my precious ones — you have me. When you walk with me, you shine — because whoever follows me will never walk in darkness, but will have the light of life.*[1] *Just as I helped you, in turn you can help others.*

If I'm ever tempted to lose sight of what a sacred privilege it is to be sent out by God to find and rescue his lost sheep, I just remember the urgency and panic I felt when it was my own child who was lost.

part 4

GOD KNOWS MY
DESTINY

chapter 8

Awakened

On a sunny day in May, a German friend of mine and I drove through beautiful green fields to a place I'd wanted to visit for years, yet dreaded: Auschwitz Birkenau, the largest of the Nazi concentration and extermination camps. From 1942 until late 1944, transport trains delivered Jews here from all over Nazi-occupied Europe. More than one million people died here, most of them gassed. Others died from starvation or disease or were worked to death by forced labor, sickened with infectious disease, executed, or tormented by medical experiments.

Since high school, I'd read books, seen movies, and visited Holocaust museums in several countries around the world. I even studied German economic history for three years at the University of Sydney. For some reason, I'd always had an over-whelming interest in World War II history, particularly in what happened to the Jewish people. Now I found myself on the same road they had traveled, on my way to what was for many of them a final destination.

Auschwitz wasn't what I expected. We passed villagers

working rolling fields of green under a blue, blue sky. Birds flitted above the grass. A stately line of birch trees lined the horizon. The countryside was beautiful and serene.

As we arrived at the camp, the cynical motto *ARBEIT MACHT FREI* (WORK SETS YOU FREE) wrought in iron at the top of the arched entry stopped us. Though the day was sunny, I felt chilled to my bones. I stared for what seemed an hour. Just seventy years ago, people streaming in by the hundreds of thousands to their death were greeted by this false sign of hope.

The camp had been turned into a giant museum, a reminder of the horrors that people could inflict upon each other. My friend and I walked through the brick buildings. Photographs of prisoners in ill-fitting striped pajamas lined the walls, along with photos of Nazis measuring people's heads in an attempt to show biological ethnic differences.

A sickening ache began in my stomach.

I turned a corner and was stopped by a large pile of shoes, gathered after the prisoners were told to remove them. There were hundreds of shoes here, worn and scuffed, all shapes, all styles and sizes. They were just shoes — and yet they were also so much more. I imagined them on the feet of my daughters; I imagined them on my husband, parents, brothers, me. I imagined where those shoes had gone when worn by the people who had worn them here. Probably the same kinds of places they'd have gone if worn by me and the people I knew and loved: work, parties, worship, home. And then they had taken the longest walk of all, to this place, only to be taken off just before stepping into a death chamber.

I stood before those shoes a long time and wept.

When I finally moved on, I came upon a display of suitcases, all with names on them: some stamped, embossed, on metal plates, others roughly scribbled across the side. I wondered about the people who bore those names, who had carried these cases, probably not knowing where they were going. What belongings had they packed? Had they packed hurriedly, urged along by armed soldiers with bayonets fixed, or had they packed slowly, in private, agonizing over every choice of what to leave behind? There were small suitcases, children's suitcases, like those my daughters pack when we travel. Had the children packed their own belongings? A favorite toy? Snacks? A pretty dress, a favorite pillow?

I walked to the next display, a huge pile of hair that had been shaved from the heads of the prisoners. Like sheep, the people had been shorn and stripped of garments and possessions. Next they were relieved of physical aids: eyeglasses, hearing aids, braces, artificial limbs, dental plates; these things were sold or used in sundry ways.

These piles of possessions belonged to only a few of those who'd been transported here, perhaps the last group. And Auschwitz was only one of the many death camps throughout Nazi Germany during the five years of World War II. Human life had no value in this place. People were publicly beaten and shot. Six million Jewish people were exterminated because of their ethnicity alone.

I was seeing the evidence, yet could not quite comprehend it.

My friend and I walked outside to get some fresh air. Across the courtyard sat many more brick buildings that we still had not entered. Each was full of more stories of horror, pain, loss, and injustice. How could one human being do this to another? How could so many people—an army—do this to a whole nation?

Eventually we walked into the next building where a display showed how each prisoner who came into Auschwitz had a number tattooed across his or her arm. From that point on, that number became their identity; they were never again to be called by name. The numbers dehumanized them, desensitized the guards to them. How much easier for the guards to ignore suffering when it did not have a name, when it was merely a number. People like Anne Frank and Corrie ten Boom became simply numerals on a list, no longer living breathing human beings. The prisoners didn't know it at the time, but the Nazis planned to eventually cross off each number from the reams of pages.

My feet felt leaden, my spirit deflated. I shuffled to the next stop, the crematorium, and read a detailed description of how it was fed.

I looked to my friend, who bore the same bewilderment and shock on her face. For a long time we stood there. We could not talk of it.

NO LONGER DISTANT

For the next hour, we made our way somberly through more of the camp. Soon we came to the train station and tracks, where, for most prisoners, the hell of camp began. Cattle cars stopped here and, once the doors opened, the people who had been crammed into each one piled out. They had been shipped, like livestock, from all across Europe. Here at the station, they were separated into lines and herded through the horrible building we'd just seen.

What would I have done, stepping into the light from that dark, windowless cattle car? Would I have cowered in fear? How would I have handled the constant gnaw of hunger? What would it be like to live in the huts full of the stench of human waste, not knowing from one second to the next if you would live or die — not knowing at what moment the guards might single you out for abuse, extra work, torture — or worse? What would I have thought, seeing the smoke billow from the chimney of the crematorium?

The helplessness, the despair, the instinct to protect oneself, the suffocating fear — those all became real to me that day.

We think of it as ancient history — but it happened during the lifetimes of our parents or grandparents. How different, I thought, to stand here and imagine this than to read of it in a book or see movies of these events. I thought of *The Hiding*

Place by Corrie ten Boom, who tried to survive here and help her sister and others endure, but in the end barely lived herself. I thought of Dietrich Bonhoeffer, the German Lutheran pastor who joined the resistance movement during the war to stop more people from being sent to the camps, but was arrested and hanged. I thought of all the arms tattooed here. Suddenly the accounts of this place no longer seemed distant, disconnected, or far removed from my life. Every person killed during the Holocaust seemed to crowd around me. Real people, not just numbers—anymore than I was merely adoptive case number 2508 of 1966. I, too, had once been only a number. The oppression they faced became tangible.

History always has a context. There were many people who shut their eyes and allowed this to happen around them. They continued living comfortable lives while others were ripped from any normal existence and sent to a hell on earth—tortured, tormented, and killed for no reason other than their heritage, their genes, their associations. *What would I have done?* I wondered. *Would I have summoned the courage to stand up against the Nazis? Would I have risked my life to save others?*

I mentioned in chapter one that I experienced my *Schindler's List* moment when I sat with Mary and Nadia and twelve other women rescued from human trafficking in Greece. But I experienced something like it, something incredibly powerful, on this day almost two years before that moment, in Auschwitz—an apt setting for such an experience. I felt a powerful and unshakable conviction that I could not continue to sit on the sidelines. Would I be able to persevere even unto death, as Bonhoeffer had? I did not know. All I knew was that I could no longer turn my back on human suffering, on injustice, on those who cried out in pain and terror. I had to stand up and be counted.

I looked to heaven and whispered a prayer, a vow. "God, help me not to close my eyes to other people's horror or ignore injustice. Help me fight the injustice you hate. Help me value people and speak up for those who have been silenced. God, you have loved, chosen, and healed me, and I want to help others be set free. If anything—anything!—like this happens in my lifetime, help me not to sit back and pretend it does not concern me."

And then I sensed God saying something directly to me: *Christine, right now, all over the world, in too many lives, something like this is happening. I am going to awaken you to things you did not know were taking place.*

My friend and I left Auschwitz that day with heavy hearts. Haunted by the horrors of the camp, I would never be the same. It was as if God nudged me to wake up from sleepwalking through life, to open my eyes to the living nightmare of others.

"I HAVE MORE FOR YOU TO DO"

I had always been passionate about my work as an evangelist. I loved teaching and preaching, bringing the good news of Christ to people. But now, while I couldn't exactly put my finger on it, I knew there was more. I felt that God was drawing me deeper still, stirring something within me that I had intuitively known but never understood. There is no distinction between preaching and doing for Jesus. They are the wings on the same plane of faith. "Faith without works is dead" (James 2:26 NKJV).

I had always envisioned those who fought for justice as the heroes written about in books—other people in other countries, living in different days. Though I'd studied about the Holocaust and other horrific events, those events seemed distant in time and place. Other atrocities did too: the Rwandan genocide in 1994, during which an estimated eight hundred thousand people were mass murdered in just one hundred days; the Cambodian genocide, during which almost two million people died through political executions, starvation, and forced labor. Until that day in Auschwitz. God had to reach into my life and awaken me to the pain of others before I could feel the powerful need to go—before I could *want* to go, rather than feeling obligated like Eeyore in the *Winnie the Pooh* books I read to my girls—"Oh dear, time to get up now. I guess I have to get to work."

After Auschwitz, something had changed. I was aware of the need to fight for justice in a way I had not been before. I felt energized to rise to what God was calling me to do.

Jesus proclaimed, "The Spirit of the Lord is on me, because he has anointed me to preach good news to the poor. He has sent me to proclaim freedom for the prisoners and recovery of sight for the blind, to set the oppressed free" (Luke 4:18). This Scripture gripped me now like never before. The word *me* kept resounding in my heart. The spirit of the Lord was upon *me*. He had anointed *me*. I sensed that something new would be required of me, of *me*—not someone else. Often, I had included this very Scripture in my teaching, using it to encourage our corporate responsibility as the church to set people free. But on my visit to Auschwitz, something awakened within me that internally shifted the emphasis from *we* to *me*. God seemed to be saying: *This new love and this new sense of purpose I've put within you are for a reason. Rise up. Get ready. I have more for you to do.*

God wanted me to rise, ready to go, as Jesus had gone on my behalf—out of love, walking wide awake through this world, seeing one prisoner yearning to be free, and then another, and another. God did not want me staying in bed, resting while a battle rages around me, fought by others. He wanted me to go—and he wanted me to go *undaunted*. There are so many daunting things in the world that we must overcome: daunting needs, daunting enemies, daunting obstacles. Only the undaunted—the undaunted *in Christ*—will be able to triumph over them.

This is what he wants for me.

And he wants the same for you.

AWAKENED AND ALARMED

My eyes, that day, were opened to how, by doing nothing when others suffer, we add to their injury. Where once I saw persecutors as in another place, of another time, I now saw myself standing beside them, while those who suffer stare back at us. The oppressed do not see too much difference between those who would keep them down and those who do nothing to help. There is no in-between.

We who live in privileged conditions don't worry about basic survival. We don't live in fear for our safety during the simple tasks of daily life. But this is not the way much of the world lives. The world in the twenty-first century is not okay. Drought, war, slavery, drugs, flooding, earthquakes, terrorism, violence, infirmity, lack of medical help, injustice because of gender or race, embargoes, disease, debt, famine, unchecked inflation, absence of the rule of law, refugee status, forced migration — the traumas around the globe are many and varied. Food, water, safety, and protection are just dreams for far too many, the lack of them a daily nightmare. So many people on the earth today spend their days simply trying to stay alive.

People not unlike you and me, made in God's image, are suffering and trapped all over the world right now. Do you feel disconnected from these tragedies being inflicted on people around the world, just because many of them live in different countries, somewhere "over there," or because you hear about them only on TV or in radio reports? So did I, once, but I've been unable to since that day. How often do you, as I used to, switch TV channels with your remote when the channel you'd been watching confronts you with some ugly tragedy — or even turn off the television lest you feel some guilt? The people living in those situations can't turn off their pain or the reality of their circumstances as easily as we turn off our TVs. How could I have ever thought that this had nothing to do with me? Were these people not loved by God, simply because they live in a different country? Were they not chosen by God, simply because their skin is a different color? Could God not heal them and give them a life beyond their past? Did they not matter as much to him as I did—as you do? Does God not know their name, as he knows mine? Does he not know their pain, or their fear? Doesn't God have a destiny in place for each one?

We all know the answer. "Whatever you did for one of the least of these brothers and sisters of mine, you did for me," Jesus said (Matthew 25:40).

If all that I had been preaching about God for years was true, then why couldn't I, wouldn't I, didn't I go and do something? I could not do everything, of course. But I could no longer do nothing. What was I waiting for?

How asleep we have been! Our disconnection does not make the abuses in this world, the injustices, any less.

So many people in the world face oppression in so many different forms. They are trapped by fear, stuck in horrible places, stripped of identity and belonging, disconnected, and disenfranchised. Single moms and single dads are trying to make family on their own: playing both roles as nurturer, provider, disciplinarian, taxi driver, home manager, play-buddy, spiritual leader, until they are exhausted, worked to death in spirit, used up and emotionally wrung out. Many people are alone, having everything they need to live except companionship—isolated, tormented, restless, anxious, hopeless, fearful. Others wonder how they are going to pay their mortgage, or put their kids through school. They wonder if anyone cares if they live or die. Runaway kids are looking for love and a next meal and a safe place to sleep, ever afraid and ever in pain, hopeless. Addicts held hostage by a drug or a bottle, in a humiliating search for the means to get those things, experience emptiness and shame between fixes, subject to horrible twists and turns in body and mind, inflicted by their drugs.

I had been asleep. Now God had awakened me so that I could rise ready to what he was calling me to do.

EYES WIDE OPEN, FAITH ACTIVATED

The apostle Paul writes to the Ephesians, "Wake up, sleeper, rise from the dead, and Christ will shine on you. Be very careful, then, how you live — not as unwise but as wise, making the most of every opportunity, because the days are evil" (Ephesians 5:14 – 16).

When we are asleep, injustice and pain can run rampant across the earth, but we may not even see or know of the nightmare someone else is living. Once we've been awakened, we can see the evil and respond. We are up, alert, ready to take the first or next step, ready to make a difference.

What does it mean, exactly, to be in the world, awake, eyes wide open, faith activated?

We Look Around Where We Are

Every day, there are situations in our normal routines that require us to be the light of Christ in darkness. Waking up spiritually is not just about participating in life-changing efforts of worldwide importance, such as stopping genocide. It is walking through our lives wide awake. It is rising ready where we are, with what we have. It is seeing people where they are and meeting their need.

For some of us, that means being a better spouse and parent, a kinder neighbor, a more engaged church member. It means seeing the world more with God's ever-awake eyes and being Jesus' hands and feet wherever we go. It means looking actively, daily, for practical ways to help people. For others it means doing what we can to stop horrific injustices such as genocide and human trafficking.

For each of us, rising ready means seeing our neighbors, understanding the needs right in front of us, and reaching out to whatever need presents itself. It means seeing others instead of always looking out for ourselves. It means offering grace to the server at the restaurant who forgets to turn in our order, causing us to have to wait another fifteen minutes before we get our food.

Is there any one of us who can't, in truth, easily forgo two lattes a week in order to sponsor a child through our church's missions program?

Rising ready may mean giving a friend who just lost a job a Starbucks card or buying her lunch, offering to do some shopping for a neighbor trapped at home with a screaming newborn, taking the time to listen to a heartbroken friend whose husband was just diagnosed with cancer. It may mean going through your closet and giving clothes to the local women's shelter.

When you're fully awakened, when you're rising ready, you will find that you've been missing out on seeing some great wonders.

We Look for God to Be at Work Around Us

Asleep, we miss the thrill of seeing God at work. It's like the time Nick and I took our girls to Disneyland, and Catherine fell asleep just before the evening fireworks display. All day, she had been anticipating the show in the sky that night. But we had seen so many sights and wonders that, by evening, she was tired. We let her drift into sleep.

Later, the show in the sky over, she awoke as we were headed back to the parking lot to go home. "Mummy," she cried, "why didn't you wake me up?"

After Auschwitz, I didn't want to miss out on the amazing ways God could use me and others to change our world, to actively help shape his story on earth, to do the good works he created for us to do from the beginning of time. Jesus said to his Father, "I do not pray that You should take them out of the world, but that You should keep them from the evil one. They are not of the world just as I am not of the world. Sanctify them by Your truth; Your word is truth. As You sent Me into the world, I have sent them into the world" (John 17:15–18 NKJV).

Before being awakened, I might have missed the wonder I experienced one Friday afternoon when, in the checkout line at the grocery store, I was getting frustrated that the clerk at the register, a young girl, was taking so long. I grumbled to myself, *Can't you hurry?*

God heard my unvoiced question and nudged me. *Christine,* I heard him say, *that girl is scheduled to have an abortion on Monday.*

I was puzzled. *God, what can I possibly do? She doesn't know me! She'll think I'm crazy if I say anything to her about it!*

But God pushed harder, this time more like a shove: *If you are my hands and feet on the earth, then do the work that I would do. Do all you can to let people know that I've not abandoned them. I will do the rest.*

I looked again at the girl, scanning the items of the customer ahead of me. Suddenly I saw not just someone slowing me down, but a girl perhaps scared inside, preoccupied with a million questions, hurting, frustrated that she has to go through such ordinary motions when something so life-changing is going on inside her.

I prayed, waiting for God to give me the right words. Suddenly what I'd thought was an everyday shopping stop took on much greater significance. Much was at stake! I even felt a brief panic attack: *What if I was wrong? What if I'd been mistaken about hearing God's voice? I didn't want to hurt this girl, nor did I want to be presumptuous. Is this what it meant to be awake?*

When I got to the front of the line, I smiled at the girl as she scanned my items. I said quietly, "Excuse me. I know you might think I am crazy, but I just wanted you to know that the thing you have scheduled to do on Monday isn't the only option. There is another way. You don't have to do it."

The girl looked up at me. She began to cry.

"It's going to be okay," I told her. "Would you like to talk about it when you get off work?"

She wiped her tears. "Yes," she said. "Yes."

I asked her name.

"Katia," she said. "I'll be off work in a couple of hours."

We agreed on a place to meet, and I walked out of the store knowing that God had just wakened me to something great.

Later, after chatting with Katia, I realized God had prompted me to help save a life. He had wakened me to be his hands and feet because there are people everywhere who are hurting and dying. I never saw Katia after that afternoon, but she did allow me to pray for her and to give her a list of alternatives to abortion, with contact information. And I got the impression that she had definitely concluded that God was real—how else could someone speak openly to what she had been hiding? That had been a miracle. How could Katia doubt a God in heaven who would tell a woman on earth about what was happening in someone else's life, just so he could let her know how much he loved her—and that she was not all alone? On that afternoon, Katia felt *chosen*— which totally changed the decision she was about to make.

God had needed me there that afternoon, I realized. And he'd needed me awake and ready. How much, like Catherine sleeping through the fireworks, I would miss if I kept sleep-walking through my days.

LOOKING FOR DARKNESS

Once, in a Walmart, Nick and I bought Sophia a flashlight of her very own. Sophia flipped on the one we thought would work best, trying it out. But none of us could see even a little glow. The fluorescent lights of the store were too bright; the flashlight's meager light was swallowed up.

"Oh, Mummy," Sophia pled, "can we please go find some darkness?"

Can we please go find some darkness?

From the mouth of babes comes the wisdom of Christ.

Darkness is everywhere. We live in a world full of fear and in need of light. No one could doubt it who sat with me that day in a safe house in Greece, listening to Nadia and Mary and the others rescued from human trafficking relate their stories of treachery and horror and rape and murder. No child could doubt it who experienced, like me, abuse at the hands of trusted adults. No adult could doubt it who spent months looking euphorically ahead to the birth of a much-loved, much-anticipated child—only to be told in cold, clinical terms, "It is no longer alive." No one could doubt it who had stood, as I had, in Auschwitz, contemplating the unspeakable horrors that had been committed there. No, clearly, darkness is everywhere.

But "You are the light of the world," Jesus said.

A city on a hill cannot be hidden. Neither do people light a lamp and put it under a bowl. Instead they put it on its stand, and it gives light to everyone in the house. In the same way, let your light shine before others, that they may see your good deeds and praise your Father in heaven. (Matthew 5:14–16)

The light quenches the darkness. The light is a danger to it. The light eliminates the darkness. The darkness should be afraid of the light, because the light of Christ will eat it up. Just as morning follows night, the light of Christ is always coming. As his hands and feet, we are the force that conquers the dark. We hold the truth that wipes out fear.

Keep your eyes on me, Jesus says. His presence in the darkness, in the face of the most primal, serious danger, vanquishes fear. Scripture promises, "Perfect love casts out fear" (1 John 4:18 NKJV). And it does. You see him, not the evil or the danger, but the love and the light. And you discover something that will change your life and the life of everyone you touch.

Once fear no longer controls you, and Christ is walking by your side, you are undaunted—and eager to go find some darkness.

BEING THE LIGHT OF THE WORLD

The prophet Isaiah says: "Arise, shine, for your light has come! And the glory of the LORD is risen upon you. For behold the darkness shall cover the earth, and deep darkness the people; but the LORD will arise over you. And His glory will be seen upon you" (Isaiah 60:1–2 NKJV).

God's glory is upon us. It can break through the darkest night. It is in us ready to burst out and overwhelm the darkness. This is what light does. It makes the darkness disappear. It edges out the black, overtakes it, gobbles it up, and eats it away. That is why God brings us each new morning. But although the light and the power are God's, he wants us to partner with him in bringing light into the dark places where oppressors try their best to shut people away in darkness.

We can get worn down by the needs in this world, and wearied by them, God knows. We need sleep, rest, restoration, recuperation. That's why God gives us the end of a day, and he doesn't begrudge us our rest. He doesn't want us to come to the end of ourselves and be defeated and enslaved in a spiritual Auschwitz, tormented, thinking it is *the work we do* that sets us free, so that we have to get back up on the treadmill and do more, be more. No, he doesn't want us to burn the candle at both ends so that we end up lethargic, fatigued, burned up, and burnt out. To do that is to walk into the lie that was wrought in iron over the arched entrance of Auschwitz—to be held captive by the idea that work sets us free. This is not what God meant when he said in Isaiah 1:12: "Why this frenzy of sacrifices?" (MSG)

Working ourselves into a frenzy or tormenting others by working them to death is not freedom. It is enslavement.

But we are not slaves; we are free. And we have been freed for a purpose: to share what we've been given. The Bible tells us, "He has shown you, oh man, what is good, and what does the LORD require of you, but to do justly, to love mercy, and to walk humbly with your God" (Micah 6:8 NKVJ).

We do justly and love mercy and walk humbly with our God when we rise ready, when we get up and go out with God to partner in his purposes on the earth. Some days, that may mean nothing more than doing a dozen little things throughout your waking hours: hearing that your neighbor's husband has just walked out on her, and providing a listening ear, a casserole, and a shoulder to cry on; seeing the pain in the eyes of the girl at the checkout register; learning that someone has lost their job and their home, and opening yours to them till they can get back on their feet.

And some days, it means bigger, more dangerous tasks.

In the book of Esther, King Xerxes is persuaded by an adviser to issue an edict condemning all the nation's Jews to death. Esther, a Jew, but chosen by King Xerxes as his queen, seems uniquely positioned to persuade the king to withdraw the edict—and, in fact, is urged to do so by Mordecai, who says, "Who knows but that you have come to your royal position for such a time as this?" (Esther 4:14)

Flying home from my visit to Auschwitz, I felt much the same: Who could say that I had not been born into a reasonably affluent and free society for such a time as this? For a time when I could see the injustice and crying need so common throughout the world and stand up to combat it?

You and I have opportunities every day to combat the darkness, the evil, that surrounds us in every country, every corner of the world. The opportunities, in fact, are countless, and the needs are desperate.

Let my *Schindler's List* moment ignite a similar moment in you. As God reminded me that day I stood in Auschwitz: As hard as it may be to believe, the crimes against God's creation, against humanity, are no less egregious today than during the days the ovens were burning at Auschwitz, and those who perpetrate them no less cruel. Genocide, slavery, murder, rape, exploitation of the helpless—those things exist throughout the world, not just in concentration camps. And they exist now—not just in history.

Whoever saves one life saves the entire world.

The darkness surrounds us, and it is growing. But *you* are the light to combat that darkness. As am I. Together, with God's help, let's beat back the darkness for just one life. And then one more, and one more . . .

chapter 9

Divine Interruption

A person's steps are directed by the LORD" (Proverbs 20:24).

I was about to find out, if I didn't already know, just how true that verse really was.

It was in 2007, twenty-one months before the safe-house meeting with Mary, Nadia, and the other women rescued from human trafficking in Greece that I related at the beginning of the book. I knew very little about human trafficking, nor was it at all on my mind as I flew to Greece. I had long yearned to minister in Greece, and now I had the chance—I'd been invited to speak at a women's conference there. I was wonderfully excited about it ...

... and had absolutely no idea yet that God had something much bigger in mind.

I'd come off the plane in Thessaloniki, ready to grab my bags and get to my hotel room for a shower, a meal, and some sleep. After all, it's a thirty-three-hour trip from Australia (via Singapore and London), and I have not yet mastered the art of sleeping in an upright position with a screaming child as background music. But the baggage carousel lurched 'round and 'round, empty—not a suitcase, duffel bag, or box in sight.

What's the holdup? I wondered. *Where are our bags?* I looked over at my fellow bleary-eyed travelers. There weren't many of us. This was the airport's final flight for the night. The other passengers began to shuffle restlessly; some moved off to look for help. My stomach grumbled, reminding me I hadn't eaten in several hours.

"Ladies and gentlemen," a voice from behind announced. (This was one of those times I was grateful that, as a child, I'd spoken Greek before I spoke English.) "There is a malfunction with the conveyor equipment that unloads your luggage from the airplane. We're working to repair it as quickly as possible. In the meantime, we are removing your luggage manually. It will take at least another half-hour before we can get your things to the carousel. Thank you for your patience."

Groans sounded all around. I understood. I was tired too. *But*, I reminded myself, *I was in Greece!* This visit was a dream come true. For almost twenty years, I had been praying for the right opportunity to work with the church in Greece, and I knew this women's conference was it. I have always had a deep love and passion for this nation—one that exceeded even my love of feta cheese and olives. After four planes and stops at four airports across the world, I was on the verge of doing something I'd worked toward and dreamed about for so long. *What's another half-hour?* I thought. *I'm here!*

The people around me weren't so congenial. Some passengers drifted away from the carousel, grumbling—probably in search of coffee or a restaurant, though at this hour nothing was open. Others sat tiredly in corners, clearly put out by the inconvenience and now turning to their own muted conversations.

Tired of sitting, and desperate to stretch my legs, I walked around the small baggage-claim area. This airport seriously needed renovation. Paint peeled off the walls. Corners were scuffed from too many slams by suitcases and luggage carts. Everything seemed so old. *It's little wonder,* I thought, *that the baggage removal equipment has broken down. I don't think they've done anything to keep up the place since the apostle Paul landed by boat.* I smiled at my own joke—the first smile I'd cracked since landing.

That's when I noticed a series of posters plastered along the length of one wall, each featuring the photos of beautiful children and young women, with one word stamped in capital letters across the top and bottom of each poster.

Missing

At front and center of the long line of posters was the wide-eyed, sweet face of three-year-old Madeleine McCann. Madeleine, the precious little girl discovered missing from her bed in Portugal, whose disappearance the international media had been covering non-stop for months.[1]

My heart wrenched. I thought of my own two daughters. Madeleine was between the ages of my firstborn, who was five, and my baby, fourteen months old. It would be early morning at home. They would be just waking up. *Oh God,* I prayed, *keep them safe. Protect our home.*

I looked back at Madeleine's picture and thought of her parents, waking up to discover that their child was no longer in the bed into which they'd tucked her and watched her fall into an innocent sleep. The word *missing* beneath her picture gripped my heart. I prayed over that picture before moving to the next poster—another little girl. And then another. The posters looked the same, yet each face struck me anew: *This one is so serene. That one is so full of life. Oh, so tiny, this one.*

Every missing person had been assigned a case number and a police contact; each poster contained instructions on what to do if you actually spotted the person in the photo. There was no other information—not whether this little girl loved dolls or that young woman sang beautifully; whether this one fidgeted and that one loved to twirl 'round and 'round. *How much these posters don't say*, I thought. *And what does "missing" mean anyway? Was this girl abducted, as is suspected in Madeleine's case? Was she taken and murdered?* I shuddered and tried to shake off the idea. *Did that one run away? Had there been a natural disaster that buried some of these children under the rubble? Was this one taken hostage?*

For more than thirty minutes I moved from poster to poster, studying the faces, wondering how I would feel if one of my daughters went missing. It was a thought I could not bear. I desperately wanted to wrap my arms around my girls and hold them close. *These photographs should be in beautiful frames on a mantle, or in the pages of a family photo album on a coffee table*, I thought. *They shouldn't be plastered coldly here, taped across the peeling paint of an airport wall.*

Suddenly, the boom and rumble of the baggage carousel interrupted my thoughts.

"Finally!" several passengers exclaimed in chorus.

I turned to see the baggage claim area come to life again. I waited as everyone else got their luggage, and just when I had given up all hope of ever seeing my bags again, there they were.

MISSING SOMETHING

As soon as I left the baggage claim, Maria and her husband, Dimitri, the pastors hosting the conference, rushed to grab my bags, apologizing for the delay, assuring me that they would soon give me a feast that would make me forget the inconvenience. In true Greek form, a meal would be the answer to any problem and the quickest remedy for jet lag.

So we drove to a restaurant where several leaders in their church were waiting to welcome me with fellowship and food. *Of course, we would be having dinner at midnight*, I thought, again smiling. *I am in Greece!* Although I was deliriously tired, I didn't want to offend my hosts. I had been taught to respect the customs of people in any country I visited, and I would just have to find my second, third, and fourth wind.

Over dinner, we chatted about the state of the church in Greece, and my new friends shared how they hoped this conference would be a defining moment for the women of their city. But as we discussed details about the week ahead, I found myself drifting in thought to those posters at the airport. The faces of those children and young women kept interrupting my thoughts. I picked up my coffee cup and rested its hot lip along my jaw and cheek for a moment. Finally, I could stand it no longer. I had to ask the question that had burned inside me for more than an hour.

"Have you seen all those posters of missing people at the airport?" I asked.

"Yes," Maria answered. Everyone else nodded.

"Why are there so many missing children and young women?"

"Mmm," Maria responded, quickly swallowing a bite just taken. "It's suspected that they were kidnapped, which seems to happen frequently these days. It's so tragic." She paused. "We don't know what else we can do other than pray for them."

A few seconds of quiet followed her comment, and then the conversation drifted back to the conference. I joined in, but could not shake from my mind the faces on those posters. I had come to minister to the women of Greece who would attend this conference, and I was excited about that—but my heart had now been stirred and my thoughts interrupted by the faces of those who would not be at the conference.

By the faces of the missing.

IT'S NOT BUSINESS — IT'S PERSONAL

A few hours later, in the dark hours of the morning, I came awake suddenly, shaken. I blinked open my eyes, even though I was still exhausted. It took me a minute, in my jet leg, to think where I was—*the hotel room. Yes. Thessaloniki.* My own tossing about had roused me. I fluffed my pillow and turned over to try once again to fall asleep.

But instead, my mind kept replaying the faces from the posters. There would be no more sleep tonight. I sat up and threw back the covers. God seemed to want my attention, and now he had it.

Jesus' story of the Good Samaritan was on my mind, because I was going to preach on it in a few hours. I knew the passage by heart. I'd read and heard this story many times before, and had reviewed and studied it over recent months for my talks for this conference. *But read it again*, God nudged. So I turned to Luke 10:30–37 (NKJV):

> *A certain man went down from Jerusalem to Jericho, and fell among thieves, who stripped him of his clothing, wounded him, and departed, leaving him half dead.*

I thought of the many people today who are in situations just like this man's. Hurt and wounded in different ways, people are lying on the side of so many different roads — people left behind by abuse, addictions, imprisonments, loss, famine, disease, violence, tyranny, and oppression. People broken by injustice and stripped of their belongings, dignity, identity, and self-worth.

I continued to read:

> *Now by chance a certain priest came down that road. And when he saw him, he passed by on the other side. Likewise a Levite, when he arrived at the place, came and looked, and passed by on the other side. But a certain Samaritan, as he journeyed, came where he was. And when he saw him, he had compassion. So he went to him and bandaged his wounds, pouring on oil and wine, and he set him on his own animal, brought him to an inn, and took care of him.*

He went to him? For some reason, as many times as I'd heard this story, those words had never registered like they did now. I went back over that phrase: *So he went to him. So he went to him.*

Like a film reel looping over and over, the idea replayed in my mind.

At first, I couldn't understand why those five words jumped out at me with such force. Defensively, I asked, "Lord, don't I spend my life going to broken people? After all, haven't I just traveled more than thirty-three hours across the globe to come and speak life, hope, and liberty to those who are spiritually and emotionally bound and hopeless?"

Read the passage again, Christine, I heard the Lord whisper.

I did, and this time I read more slowly. This time it was as though I had been blind the many times I'd read this story, but now I could see. It seemed in this moment as though scales fell from my eyes.

Before, I had always thought of myself as the Good Samaritan. After all, I was an itinerant evangelist who spent most of the year on the road, literally making it my business to go to *them*—the broken and those dying in ditches—perhaps in ditches of their own making, perhaps thrown there by the cruelty of others. I had a jam-packed schedule, carefully planned, all audiences and destinations carefully selected. Now I was reading between the lines of Jesus' story, and I was hearing him ask: *But what about those you had not planned to go to, those whom you have been walking past for years, on the way to those you'd chosen to reach? What about the young women and children on the posters at the airport?*

Nowhere in Jesus' story does it say that the priest or the Levite were bad people. But they were busy people, religious people. They were so consumed with keeping their schedules, appointments, and commitments that they ended up walking past someone they should have helped. The man lying on the side of the road was an *interruption* to their ministry, rather than the object of it.

Oh Lord, I asked myself, *how many posters in how many airports have I walked past, seeing but never noticing? Am I really any different from the priest who, on his way to some priestly duty, saw the man lying wounded and broken and simply passed by on the other side? Was I any different from the Levite, who looked, saw, and then went on his way?*

And then the Lord said to me, *Christine, the only difference between the Samaritan and the religious people was that the Samaritan actually crossed the street. The Samaritan was willing to have his plans interrupted so that he could assist the man. The Samaritan stooped down to lift up the broken one. Stopping and stooping are different. Compassion is only emotion—until you cross the street. Compassion means action. You go to them.*

I wanted to weep.

I saw in my mind Jesus, who not only crossed the road from heaven to earth, not only stopped to see our hurts and heal our wounds, but then stooped to bear the cross for us, and looked at us, and lifted that cross to the hill where he was nailed to it in our stead.

STOPPED BEFORE WE STOOP

On my visit to Auschwitz, related in the previous chapter, I had been jarred awake by the stunning and appalling evidence of people's inhumanity to people; I had cringed and shuddered in a flood of empathy with those who had suffered unspeakably in that place. And although I had not fully understood on that day what God was doing in me, I saw clearly and powerfully for the first time a multitude of needs around the world—needs related to injustice, to poverty, to oppression, to circumstance, to disaster.

Now God was taking me the next step. It is one thing to be awakened to injustice and quite another to be willing to be inconvenienced and interrupted to do something about it. Now God was reaching into my life not just to make me aware, but to interrupt me and turn my steps toward those in need so that, like the Samaritan, I could not only stop—but stoop to help them.

After all, I had stared into the faces on those posters in the airport. How can you turn and walk away from the oppressed and wounded once they stare back into your eyes?

I couldn't, not sitting that night in my hotel room, my Bible in my lap, the story of the Good Samaritan in my head, the image in my heart of Jesus struggling up the road to the cross. And I couldn't the next week, either, when I got back on a plane to fly home.

Though I hadn't returned to the baggage claim area in Thessaloniki, the faces on those posters imprinted themselves on my mind nevertheless. They had interrupted my thoughts all week, and they were with me all the way home.

I could not go on with "ministry as usual." I was going to follow in the footsteps of the Samaritan, of Jesus. I was going to reach out to these missing ones — only I had no idea how or when and with what.

For months, I searched for answers. I made phone calls. I asked questions. I did all kinds of research. I discovered that the faces I'd seen on those posters were not just randomly missing people or runaways. They were, allegedly, victims of human trafficking.

Human trafficking. The very term was so ugly and serious and shattering. As I write this, the current estimates from the United Nations are that *twenty-seven million people* have been lured, kidnapped, forced or taken *as slaves* upon our earth — not yesterday, not in some other time, but now, today. Twenty-seven million individuals with faces and family, bought and sold like goods and commodities, with no voice, no rights. Traded for money and either sex or forced labor. *How can any one person reach all of them? How can I be sure, Lord, that you're leading me to this deep, dark ditch, where awaits not one Samaritan but twenty-seven million slaves? How can I free them all?*

No sooner had I formed that thought than I had to laugh at myself. After all, I of all people was acquainted with what numbers could do. Wasn't I number 2508? Hadn't someone crossed the street to see me and help me? Hadn't someone heard my cry, felt my pain, and chosen not to walk on by but lift me out of my brokenness into the loving arms of Jesus?

I refused to be overwhelmed by the numbers.

That's right, I sensed God urging me on. *And you have already helped so many in the ditches before you. Now cross the street to those others. Stop. Stoop.*

Yes, I realized. A divine interruption is different from an awakening. God had gently led me to an awakening at Auschwitz, nine months before my trip to Thessaloniki. Now he was interrupting my ministry schedule so that I could do something even more impactful. He had prepared even more good works for me to do, if I was willing. He was showing me that the Samaritan not only *went* to the broken one, but he did more: He gave medical supplies and transportation, and he paid for restoration. The Samaritan, the true neighbor, is the one who gives not only his time, but his talent and treasure too.

I was excited. I wanted to do this. I, who had been rescued from a dark place and restored, could help set others free.

And no sooner was I inspired to go, than I immediately began to think of one hundred reasons I was unable — one hundred reasons to be *daunted*.

Isn't that human nature? We're roused to do something, and then we immediately forget the one reason that we are capable of doing anything at all. When I initially discovered the magnitude of the problem of human trafficking across the earth, I, like most other people, was so overwhelmed that I began to compile a list for God of all of the reasons I, a forty-year-old mother of two living on the other side of the world, could not possibly do anything that would significantly change the statistics. I don't know what your "but God" list might be. Are these items on it?

- But God, I don't know enough about the issue.
- But God, I'm not educated enough to get involved.

- But God, I'm not skilled enough.

- But God, I already have enough on my plate.

- But God, I have a family.

- But God, it's too dangerous.

- But God, I'm too old to start something new.

- But God, I'm too young to be taken seriously.

- But God, this will tip the scales of balance in my life.

But God ... the list goes on. Does it sound familiar? This is the same kind of daunting self-doubt—or just plain excuses—that we've stubbed our toes on throughout the book.

Maybe a list like this is what kept the priest going on his way. *But I'm not a doctor. I can't help. That man's brokenness is bigger than I know how to tend. I should go on to those I do know how to help.*

Maybe the Levite, who came closer, thought the same: *This is way too big for me. I'm not strong enough to lift this fellow. I can't carry him. I don't belong in this world. I need to stay focused on what I already know God wants me to do.*

Maybe you see a rise in teen pregnancy in your community, but you're a mom of elementary-aged daughters and think: *What do I know about teenagers anyway? Why would they listen to me? How could I ever help them when I can't even keep up with my housework, let alone find homes or resources for teen moms and their babies?*

Maybe you see a TV commercial highlighting the plight of starving children in Africa, and wonder, *What difference could I possibly make on the other side of the world? I'm just trying to keep my own kids on track!*

How easy it is to let the depth of the ditch or the severity of the brokenness stop a good work before we even stoop down to do it. How often we pray for God to use us for his purpose—and then when he interrupts our lives to answer our prayer, we list all our inadequacies.

I protested, *How can I alone reach twenty-seven million people?* But all along, God was simply asking, *Will you cross the street and reach out to one?*

He does not ask us to cross the street because we actually have the capacity in and of ourselves to rescue hurting people. He asks because he does.

He does not ask, *Are you capable?* He asks, *Are you willing?*

NO GIFT TOO SMALL

When God invites us to cross the street, he never asks us to go alone. He goes along. He goes ahead. He's by our side. We know this because he has promised to never leave us nor forsake us (Hebrews 13:5). The wonderful (but easily overlooked) reason we can stride into our destiny confident and undaunted is not that we are so great — *but that the God who is within us is so great!* "The one who is in you is greater than the one who is in the world" (1 John 4:4).

What does this mean for us? It means that while we may think we don't have enough time, money, resources, or know-how for the task, God will use what we have.

It's important to remember this, because otherwise we may be so convinced that our contribution will be so small, insignificant, even inconsequential, that we decide to do nothing.

Jesus has always used small things to make a big difference. In Matthew 14, he used a young boy's lunch to feed five thousand people. I'm sure that if you'd asked the boy that morning if he had brought enough food to feed the whole crowd, he'd have laughed — "With five little loaves of bread and two fishes? There are thousands of people here! We'd be lucky to each get a piece the size of a pebble." If you had asked him what he was doing, then, offering his lunch to Jesus, he might well have said, "He might be hungry — and even though I don't have enough lunch for everyone, I have enough for one person. I'll let him eat my lunch."

But once he'd given that small gift to Jesus, Jesus used it to do something far beyond what that boy might have imagined or expected. And that's exactly what he does with our small gifts.

Whatever we receive from God is what he asks that we give to someone else. This is what Jesus meant when he said, "Freely you have received; freely give" (Matthew 10:8).

I saw the power of this the time my own Sophia and I were walking down a crowded street. I had a full day, but had promised to let her accompany me on it—a special treat for both of us. I was racing the clock, determined to make it to Starbucks before a meeting. We'd been running hard and fast all that day to keep appointments, to get things done, and I needed a pick-me-up. Images of tall cups of seventy percent foam, extra-hot, skim cappuccinos were dancing in my head.

Sophia, on the other hand, would have been happy just to walk along and look at everything: the shop-window displays, the flower and tree pots outside the buildings, the cars parked alongside the curb. But I was on a mission.

Suddenly I realized that Sophia's hand was no longer in mine. I grabbed at the air, reaching for her, but touched nothing. I whirled around to find her.

Just steps behind, she had stopped to kneel at the curb next to a man who appeared to be homeless. She held out to him the dollar I'd given her that morning to buy a treat for herself. She had been holding tight to that dollar the entire day. It was a treasure, a rare gift for a special day with Mummy, and she'd been trying to decide exactly how to spend it on our day downtown. Now, without hesitation, she was handing it to a stranger.

"Jesus gave me this dollar to give to you," she said.

How easily she had handed over what was so precious to her. How powerful that mere dollar became.

The man she handed it to handed it back, tears streaming down his face. "Honey," he said, "you spend that on some candy for yourself."

He had been given something much more precious than her dollar. Sophia had given her heart—and so much more. She gave him hope. She reminded him that there was goodness in this world, and grace—even from a child. She had reminded him that God would provide—even from the least and most unlikely sources. Sophia had crossed the street (or at least moved to the side of it), and God had gone with her. He used her open hand to open a stranger's heart. And he used her willing spirit on that day to show me that when we give what we have, and don't overthink it, God—the God of hope—delivers all the rest.

CULTIVATING A HEART TO CROSS THE STREET

How do you know whether something is a God interruption or a distraction from the good works you're on the road to completing? It's not always easy. These five habits help me know when the Lord is leading me to cross the street and help the one in the ditch:

1. Be Sensitive to the Spirit of God

Before I was interrupted by the girls' faces on the posters, I was already a busy wife, mom, and evangelist. I wasn't particularly looking to undertake any additional projects. But after my moment with God at Auschwitz, when I was *awakened* to the pains and needs and hurts of others around me, nine months passed before my moment in the airport at Thessaloniki, waiting for my luggage. During those nine months, I spent daily time with him in his Word and in prayer. I had a growing and inescapable sense during those months that he wanted to stretch and enlarge my life. Everywhere I went, I began to see more people in the ditch. By the time I looked at the faces of the missing, on those posters in Thessaloniki, I knew that the sudden urge I felt to go to them was more than just a passing interest. It was God interrupting me.

Listen to what God keeps bringing to your attention, what he interrupts your thoughts and your days with. In those things, you will recognize his leading.

There's no formula for confirming that when you feel such a leading, it's God's voice you're hearing. But if there is a need before you that you can easily do something about, then by all means do it! If the interruption is more significant—one that is potentially life-altering for you—then seek the counsel of your pastor, a spiritual leader, or trusted friend.

You'll find that the one in the ditch you are supposed to help is often along the way you're already going. The Samaritan crossed the street and helped the broken man, and after giving the help that was needed, he continued on his journey. He fulfilled his initial commitment—but he made time to allow himself to be interrupted to help someone else. God didn't stop me from being a wife, mother, or speaker in order to reach out to the victims of human trafficking, He asked whether I would allow myself to be interrupted—and then expanded my capacity and enlarged my sphere of influence.

2. Live Aware

Too often, when we are the answer to someone's prayer, we miss it. We stay busy going places and doing things, intent on our own agendas. When we cross a street, we're intent on getting to the other side, for instance.

What if we paid a little more attention to the older woman struggling to step down from the curb? Or the fellow trying to balance a bunch of boxes in his arms, one or more of which we could carry for him? What if we *looked* for people who need help, instead of just seeing what we want to get done or take home in the next minute?

Greet each interruption with a question: *Lord, what is it you really want from me here?*

3. Simply Step into the Moment

Don't overthink being interrupted. If we hesitate and give them the chance, our own insecurities, feelings of awkwardness, schedule, and agenda may stand in the way of the moment of interruption that God has prepared for us. Make it a habit to:

- Give an encouraging word to someone standing next to you in line.
- Acknowledge a cashier or waitress or service clerk by the name on his or her name tag, rather than treating that person as your servant.
- Make focused eye contact with those you address in any situation.
- Respond with patience to rude treatment, even though you would really much rather respond in kind.
- Drop a dollar in the homeless man's tin or save small change for donations to the neighbor child's fundraiser.

4. Pray for a Heart Change

Allow God to continually soften your heart so that it beats for what his heart beats for—people. God does not want us to fill our lives with empty, obligatory good works so that we can appease our religious conscience. He desires to transform our hearts—because it is out of our hearts that all of the issues of life flow (Proverbs 4:12). When our hearts are changed, we see things we never saw before, hear cries that we never heard before, and act out of a compassion that we did not have before.

It's so easy to stay locked in a selfish cycle of *my* time, *my* objectives, *my* plans. But ask God to transform you into his image: to see what he sees, feel what he feels, love as he loves. He promises to "give you a new heart and put a new spirit in you" (Ezekiel 36:26). In fact, he says, "I will remove from you your heart of stone and give you a heart of flesh."

5. Be Open

I always say, "Blessed are the flexible, for they shall not be snapped in two." Flexibility will enable you to keep stretching and reaching out to those who need a helping hand. That means loosening up your life enough to be ready for interruptions. Don't structure your days so rigidly that you lock out God from working with you in the middle of them.

Isn't it easy to book our calendar so full that we run from one activity to another, leaving only Wednesday evening Bible study and Sunday morning church as our times for meeting God? That's not what he wants — and not what you want either. You want him by your side through the day, and he wants that too. He longs to walk with us into each moment of every day, loving us, leading us, guiding us — and yes, gently interrupting us. Plan moments for talking to him, listening, worshiping, and praising him.

Don't wait to start. Ask him to order your steps, as he promises in Psalm 119:133. Remind yourself of Psalm 37:23 (NLT): "The LORD directs the steps of the godly. He delights in every detail of their lives." Keep an eye not just on the road ahead, but also on the ditches, as God looks to interrupt your day as he did the Samaritan's.

I'd thought God led me to Thessaloniki to speak at a conference and strengthen the church there. But he used my momentarily lost luggage and a little lost sleep to show me where he needed me next. He was interrupting not just my day, but the whole direction of my ministry. He was asking me not just to cross the street, but to think of how to reach the missing, the lost girls and young women on those posters, in the darkest, most hidden ditches across the globe.

The ones we're asked to go to are not always across the street or around the globe. Sometimes they're right under our nose and just at our elbow, as was Katia at the checkout line. And the moment we don't think we have to give? God takes even what we may, at first, offer reluctantly — and he uses it, in spite of time, on what's eternal. And the miracle that waits there in the ditch? It's the thing I possessed all along to give to Sonia or whoever else I find in the ditch. It's the thing each of us wants most of all.

Hope.

chapter 10

Facing Giants

Wait, Nick," I said into my cell. "They're making an announce-ment—I can't hear you." I lowered the phone, scooping all the contents back into my purse from where I'd dumped them in my frantic search for my phone before it stopped ringing. Impatient airline passengers detoured around me, some throwing frowns or smirks back over their shoulders, as the loud and nearly un-intelligible announcement ground to a halt. I nestled the phone against my ear again. "Hi, Babe," I said. "I can hear you now." He had gone ahead of me to Greece, and had been there a few days preparing the way. I was on my way now to meet him.

"Chris," my husband said, his tone serious. "We need to talk."

Actual phone calls always startled me anyway. Because of constant travel, I typically communicated exclusively through text and email. But Nick's somber tone unnerved me even more than usual. My stomach dropped. "Are the kids all right? Is Mum? Has anything happened?" My mind went to a dozen more horrible possibilities.

"Yes, yes, no," Nick said. "Everyone is fine. I just want to give you a heads-up about the report the consultants are going to present when you arrive because ..." He paused. "I know you are not going to like it."

Although I'd long since learned to trust Nick completely, I still didn't like surprises. And something big must be up for him to feel the need to prepare me like this for the meeting ahead, with several consultants we'd hired to help us think through the launch of our next big initiative: an international nongovernmental organization to combat human trafficking.

After my airport baggage-claim experience in Thessaloniki (chapter nine) and after about fifteen months of discussions with our senior pastors, extensive prayer, and much soul searching, Nick and I took a leap of faith. We could not ignore the international crisis of human trafficking. We could not go back to ministry as usual. We decided to take action. We believed God was asking us to start an organization to rescue, restore, and rebuild the lives of the victims of human trafficking. We called it The A21 Campaign as shorthand for "abolish injustice in the twenty-first century."

That had been only three months ago—and now, so soon, Nick was telling me he had news I wasn't going to like.

"Chris," Nick said, "after twenty-five days of extensive research, discussions with government authorities, law enforcement, legal representatives, and other nongovernment organizations—well, you're not going to believe this. The consultants have come to the conclusion that we should not start our work in Europe with an emphasis on Eastern Europe because—their words—it's certain to fail. The difficulties ahead are insurmountable."

The conclusion? I wasn't sure I was hearing this right.

We'd already known, before we even hired the consultants, that there were many reasons starting A21 in Greece didn't make sense. We knew the challenges. We had discussed them at great length. And we had decided that we could not ignore

God's call, regardless of the difficulty. That decision had already been made. We had hired the consultants to help us navigate the troubled waters we knew lay ahead of us, not to make our decision for us.

So now it was with great frustration that I heard Nick continue, "Their research suggests there are too many factors working against us for A21 to have any chance of success in Eastern Europe. There's too much corruption, and there aren't enough laws to protect the rights of victims. The women will be reluctant to testify against their abductors, since their own well-being and that of all those they love has already been threatened. Search and rescue would be extremely dangerous, because criminal networks have huge strongholds into all areas of society where we would be going. Prostitution is legal there, and awareness of human trafficking is nonexistent, so we'll have a tough time garnering support. And with the current state of the economy, our costs for an operation of this magnitude are going to be sky high. They're not convinced we'll be able to get the financial backing."

Nick was right. I didn't like what I heard—and I couldn't believe I was hearing it. "You mean after twenty-five days, all we've got is a list of how hard the challenge will be and why this can't work? And that isn't even an original list—we pointed out to them all those same problems at the initial meeting!" I was stunned. *Really? We paid good money to expensive consultants so they could help us find a way to succeed—and the only thing they can tell us is that it's impossible?*

I had not asked our consultants *if* we could run an anti-human-trafficking initiative in Greece. I had asked them *how to start*. We already knew that the odds were stacked against us. We knew the degree of darkness we would be required to enter. What we didn't know, and why we needed their advice, was where we should begin. What steps do we take? What should we prepare for, and how? Where could we find resources?

I stood in the airport, the crowd parting to pass me, listing in my mind all the things we needed to determine. And as I did, my resolve strengthened. *Of course this campaign is going to be difficult*, I thought. *If it were easy, then it would already be done. Everyone would be doing it.* To these highly experienced consultants, our idea — which we believed was *God's* idea — looked impossible. And maybe it was. But then . . .

Hadn't David defeated Goliath with a simple slingshot and one smooth rock (1 Samuel 17)? With God on our side, couldn't we too overcome the giant obstacles in our path? Like Goliath, these giants were huge. They made a lot of noise pounding their spears against their shields, and they issued a lot of threats. But he who is in us is greater than he who is in the world (1 John 4:4).

Yes, I knew that consultants were paid to turn their experience loose on our problems, and to offer their honest opinions, positive or negative. But in this case, what we needed was not help in identifying the giants. We already knew where the giants were. We needed help in finding the stones we would use to destroy them.

I straightened up to my full five feet and three inches and took a deep breath. To the world, A21 didn't make sense. But our foundation for believing it would succeed regardless trumped the world's wisdom:

- God is with us (Romans 8:31).

- God is in the business of making miracles where humans fail (Hebrews 13:5 – 6).

- God told us to go into all the world (Matthew 28:19 – 20), and he'd shown me a part of the world so dark and hidden I hadn't even known it was there, and he was not letting me forget it.

"Nick," I said loudly, "we need to tell them that God has already given us the victory. Tell them that we are well able to take the land because he is with us. Tell them that we know they're right that this makes no sense in earthly terms. Nevertheless, we will go—because God can make a way where others say there is no way."

I was more convinced than ever that we were on the right track. True, I was no clearer on *how* we were going to bring about change for those enslaved to human trafficking, but I knew we had to do it. *Thank you, God,* I prayed, *for being the God who helps us to overcome challenges and difficult circumstances, for being the God who makes a way through the wilderness and makes the crooked paths straight. Now help us figure out the next step, and the step after that.*

And just as I said *amen*, another announcement blared over the airport loudspeaker. "All passengers on Aegean Airlines flight to Thessaloniki, Greece, we are now boarding. Those on Aegean Airlines to Thessaloniki, Greece, board at gate A21."

DIFFICULT, YES

Gate A21. Sometimes God has to shout over the crowds and the clamor for us to understand that, although there will always be difficulties in this world, the one who created the universe can overcome them.

This was one of those times.

By choosing, at the exact time A21 was under fire, to have my flight leave from the gate that bore the same name as our campaign, God was subtly reminding me of who was in charge: *Yes,* he was saying, *the odds are stacked against you. Overwhelmingly, in fact. Yes, every bit of reason and all the advice you've paid for says to stop before you've even started. Yes, the giants you're facing can make you think there's no way forward. But none of those things can stop me, and when you do my will, they can't stop you, either.*

"In the world you will have tribulation," Jesus promised (John 16:33 NKJV), and added, "but be of good cheer, I have overcome the world."

God is always with us and always making a way for us to do his will, to bring his hope and change into this world. But there's so much temptation to think otherwise. You'll be asked to speak to a group but think, *I can't! I'm too shy.* You'll want to volunteer at a local shelter, but your schedule will tell you that you're too busy and cannot add one more thing. You'll want to give some money or groceries and goods to a family burned out of their home, but your checkbook says there's not enough in your account to pay even your own bills, let alone help with someone else's. You'll want to make a career change to follow what you know is your calling, yet your confidence will mutter: *Stay where you are. There are too many unknowns! It makes no sense to give up a job other people would kill for just to try for some ephemeral sense of happiness.*

Difficulty is the bully that steps into your path and tries to arm-wrestle you to the ground until you cry uncle. No matter what you're trying to do, if it's worthwhile, he will try to outshout both God and your own thoughts, confusing you. He tries to loom so large that you can only see what's right in front of you—the problems, the obstacles, and the walls. Difficulty sings an old song: Whatever it is you're trying to do will take too much time, money, risk, comfort, health, strength, willpower ...

Difficulty loves to sing about hurdles that have been around since the beginning of time.

In fact, Difficulty's tune is as old as Moses.

When Moses led the children of Israel out of slavery, Difficulty was there every step of the way, singing, "Can't, won't, don't." Pharaoh granted the people freedom, and Difficulty laughed and said that it would cost the Israelites blood (the lives of precious ones, Exodus 11), sweat (labor was increased, Exodus 5), and tears (because all kinds of plagues beset them, from frogs and flies and locusts to hail and boils and slaughtered cattle, Exodus 7–11).

Even after God got the Israelites through those things, Difficulty was singing in the distance, "It's not over!" Difficulty is like that. He hangs around. He lurks. When he saw the Israelites win their freedom, he said, "Don't think you're leaving *me* behind." He was with them at the shore of the Red Sea, and in the desert where there was no water or food and no clear path to the Promised Land.

And why? What did he want? He wanted the Israelites to stop—to return to Egypt.

What if they had? They might still be enslaved there to this day. Still building their oppressor's kingdom, and his temples, instead of God's. They would have continued to suffer injustice instead of enjoying the freedom of the Lord. They would have languished under Pharaoh's thumb instead of grabbing all that God was calling them to.

Don't let Difficulty keep you from daring to go where God wants you to go. God will make a way.

IMPOSSIBLE? NO

He made a way for the children of Israel; when Difficulty had been telling them that there was no way, God brought them into the Promised Land. He parted the Red Sea (Exodus 14), fed them bread from heaven (Exodus 16), and showed them water in the desert (Exodus 17). God made a way for them through Difficulty again and again, for more than forty years.

When the Israelites were on the verge of entering the Promised Land, God had Moses assemble a band of twelve to go and scout out what was ahead, and report back on the details (Numbers 13). God didn't have Moses ask his scouts *if* they could possess the land. He had already said he was giving them the land—that was a fact, not a possibility. What Moses asked was for them to consider *how* to go. He wanted to know: Were the people in this place strong or weak, few or many? Was the land rich or poor, the towns unwalled or fortified? Were there trees or none, good soil or worthless?

Hold Onto Where God Wants You to Go

Only two of the twelve scouts Moses sent out understood their mission. Ten came back with the report that the land was big, and the people in it even bigger (Numbers 13:28, 32). All they could see were the giants, the obstacles. Joshua and Caleb remembered what they were asked to do: not to figure out *if* they could take the land, but to find out how it was laid out and what the Israelites would need to do to possess it.

Nick and I sympathized with Moses—we felt as if we were in the same situation. We'd wanted the scouts we'd sent, the consultants, to help us figure out how best to claim what God had already given us. We were ready to go, and we knew God was with us. We just needed someone to scout the lay of the land. We needed scouts with vision, not excuses.

See the Possibilities and His Promise

When Difficulty pops up, God wants us to see and hear something more—something beyond the difficulty. Two of the scouts, Joshua and Caleb, did that. Instead of looking just at what was in front of them, they kept their eyes on God, who was higher and bigger. (God is *always* higher and bigger.) Rather than being distracted by all that looked impossible, they saw all that was possible. The song in their heads was not the old, sad song of Difficulty, but rather the song of all that God had promised. It was as if they could hear that song of jubilance they would be singing when they entered that land (Joshua 5). And instead of fixating on the problems, they remembered God's promise—a land of plenty for their people. They could see it, feel it, taste it.

"We should go up and take possession of the land," Joshua and Caleb told Moses and all the people (Numbers 13:30), "for we can certainly do it."

They knew that the same miracles that God had performed to get the children of Israel out of Egypt would suffice to take them into the Promised Land. This task was no harder, and the miracles required were no bigger. God—the same today, yesterday, and tomorrow (Hebrews 13:8)—was sufficient.

So why did only two of the twelve scouts see that the land could be theirs? Why did ten of the scouts say, "We can't attack those people; they are stronger than we are" (Numbers 13:31). Two of the men saw what God could do. Ten of the men only saw what Difficulty said they could not. And why? Because guess what was in that land? Giants! "All the people we saw there are of great size.... We seemed like grasshoppers in our own eyes, and we looked the same to them" (Numbers 13:32–33).

Then, as now, obeying God required getting past the giants.

We are well able, God tells us whenever the bully Difficulty crosses our path. With God, Psalm 18:29 promises, you can leap over a wall.

We are well able, I wanted to remind our consultants about A21. We and the consultants were walking the same path but seeing different things. They were focusing on all that we knew we were up against. They stood with us on the edge of starting something God wanted, but they missed it. The very giants over whom God was giving us victory overwhelmed them before we even got into the fight.

Get your eyes off the bully of this world, Difficulty, and onto God, who promises nothing is too difficult for him (Matthew 19:26).

Keep Going Forward a Step at a Time

You must always take a first step, and then another, and another. When God said *go*, Moses immediately chose scouts from each tribe to enter the Promised Land—there was no waiting around (Numbers 13:21–24).

Nick and I knew that God had chosen us to start A21. He kept leading us to the edge of it and saying *go*. So even when the consultants balked and said there was no way, no map, not enough supplies, we knew we had to go anyway. We had to start from where we were, with what we had, and God would provide what else we needed when we needed it. We made up our minds. It was November when the consultants delivered their dire warnings. But we decided that the team we'd had on the ground in Greece since the previous August would stay, and we would move forward with our plans to grow our legal office and open a shelter for rescued victims—the warnings of the consultants notwithstanding.

Through human eyes, many things seem impossible, Jesus told us (Matthew 19:26). "But with God all things are possible." We would trust in that promise.

Pave the Way with Prayer

As with the Israelites, the greatest giants we face are spiritual ones: Difficulty. Discouragement. Detours caused by a lack of confidence or pride or fear.

But, as Moses and Joshua and Caleb learned, those giants are best slain by a talk with God, petitioning and praising him, listening to him (Numbers 14).

Prayer allows you to knock Difficulty off its feet, even when you're on your knees. It's a power like no other, a great first option—not just a last resort. When you move into the future undaunted, miracles begin to happen. The impossible becomes possible.

Not knowing what else to do, we mobilized everyone we knew to pray through every difficulty the consultants had told us would make the success of A21 impossible.

Our first challenge was to establish a safe house for rescued victims. We'd opened our legal office in Thessaloniki and hired a lawyer and operations manager, but authorities told us it would take at least two years to get all the approvals and permits to open and operate the rescue home—and there were no guarantees that we would be given the necessary permits once our application was processed.

There was nothing to do but watch and pray, we decided.

So as we prayed, our lawyer turned in our applications and met with the regional anti-human-trafficking unit. As she shared her passion to see girls rescued and restored, a strange thing happened. She told of one of her own children who had died, and how, although she would never hold him on this earth again, she could help other parents hold their children. "Please," our lawyer said, "please help me to help others out of this pain."

The head of the regional office began to weep. In the course of her work, she had never heard such a passionate, sincere, authentic plea.

That very day, we received the necessary permit. That never, ever happens in Greece: one-day approval. And this was in December—less than a month after the negative report from the consultants! Not only did we receive the permit, we were granted premises: a safe house that was already registered was available, we were told. All we had to do was come up with the money to renovate it and pay the rent.

God not only gave us what we needed (the permit) but more (the premises).

Not surprisingly, Difficulty once again reared his head— we couldn't afford to pay the monthly rent.

Again, we turned to prayer: *Lord, make a way*. As we prayed, we received calls from people at various churches, asking how they could help support this new work.

I couldn't believe it. We'd prayed for help—and God didn't just show us where to get help. He brought it to us.

And that's how it went with each step we took to form A21. We prayed our way forward—for divine alignments, for favor, for resources, and for open doors—and where the consultants had said there was no way, God made a way. He moved hearts and paperwork and houses, and delivered not only what was needed, but more.

When the Greek authorities who conducted the investigations into human trafficking were hampered by cuts in the funding for their search-and-rescue missions, we prayed for them too.

We have a safe house, we prayed, *so please, God—bring us the girls who need help.*

"That's ridiculous," some people said. "The missing and lost don't come to you—you have to go find them—that's why we call it *rescue.*"

Earnestly we prayed, in shifts, around the clock. *God, if you want us to rescue these girls, you'll have to make a way. If the police can't fund investigations, you'll have to convict the clients to help us. Work on their hearts.*

One day a man walked into the police station with a girl who spoke only broken Greek. It turned out she had been a sex slave, and the man with her was a client. Except that after he'd gone to a brothel, paid for her services, and taken her to a designated room, he couldn't go through with what he had intended.

Why? he wondered. He had, after all, come there for that purpose, and had paid for it.

Why? the girl wondered, confused but relieved.

He couldn't explain. Instead, he asked the girl if she had registration papers, the legal requirement for all registered sex workers.

Breaking into tears, she told him her story in broken Greek. She had been trapped. She wasn't registered. She was a sex slave.

The truth broke his heart. He snuck the girl out of the brothel and took her to the police, who brought her to our safe house.

The officer helping with the transition said that, in twenty years of police work, he had never seen such a thing. It was Christmas—and we had our first client, the first woman rescued from trafficking through the ministry of A21.

Difficulty had sneered that there was no way. But God made a way. Just as he did when the pastor of our local church, Bobbie Houston, woke one morning feeling burdened for girls from the "stan" nations—Afghanistan, Kazakhstan, Kyrgyzstan, Turkmenistan, Pakistan, Uzbekistan.

She wanted to help them, but how? She summoned the Colour Sisterhood, a global sisterhood of praying women, and asked for prayer for women in the "stan" nations. In multiple time zones and every quarter of the globe, tens of thousands of women connected by social media on Twitter and Facebook prayed for girls trapped in the "stan" countries. They didn't know exactly what to pray for, but they knew who did.

Three days later, the police conducted a raid in northern Greece. Eleven girls were rescued from human trafficking; some were brought to our safe house. They were from Uzbekistan.

When they poured out their stories to us, one said, "We prayed to the God of Europe." Her companions nodded in agreement. " 'If you are real,' " the girl said they prayed, " 'if you exist, God, come and save us. We have asked Allah to rescue us and he has not. So, Jesus, if you are real, send someone to help us.' "

Coincidence?

I know otherwise. I know this was the power of prayer. When Difficulty shouts, "Impossible!" God makes a way. God says, "Done."

MY GOD IS SO BIG

That, after all, is what God does. He shows up. He speaks out. He shines. When you're convinced something is hard and difficult, when everyone tells you that it's impossible, God brings you the lost who were hidden. He paves the way for all the right permits. He leads you to the girls who were forgotten.

When the consultants we hired told us that A21 would fail in Eastern Europe, they gave us the benefit of their experience and wisdom in a way that made perfect sense to them. They believed they were telling us the truth. They made a sound case for why we could not do what we felt God was calling us to do. But when we decided to obey God, we didn't enlist him on *our* side—we joined *his* side. And God plus one is a majority. He's bigger than the bully Difficulty and greater than any giant.

When difficulties get in the way of us daring to do what God has called us to do, we must ask ourselves, *Who am I going to believe? The rational—or the supernatural? The factual—or the true?*

The Bible tells us that Moses and the Israelites, and Abraham before them, all got to the destination God had ordained for them by faith (Hebrews 11). Their journey made no sense: Leaving everything they had, the safe and familiar, for the unknown wasn't rational or explainable, definable or predictable. But the exercising of faith requires the unknown, along with the unexpected and unpredictable and outrageous.

Faith is required when you're in doubt, when you're in want, when things are difficult and unclear. "Faith," the Bible tells us, is, "confidence in what we hope for and the assurance about what we do not see" (Hebrews 11:1).

You can't touch faith, but it can move mountains. The Bible puts it this way: You may not be able to hold faith or wrap it up in a box, but it is real and powerful and can conquer kingdoms, administer justice, gain what was promised. It can shut the mouths of lions, quench the fury of flames, escape the edge of the sword, raise the long dead, end torture, and release the imprisoned (Hebrews 11:33–38). Faith can take you right where God wants you.

At times, it's possible to see life as a conflict between faith and that old bully Difficulty. And Difficulty loves to stand directly in the way, so that we see as little as possible ahead.

Which is just when we need faith.

How misleading our perspective is for the things God calls us to do. We see problems. He sees possibilities. We see difficulty. He sees destiny. We see a disheveled woman, fishing around in her purse for her phone in the hubbub of a busy airport, and God sees a person with a calling and a purpose and something big to do in a place inhabited by all kinds of giants.

There is no promise too hard for God to fulfill. When our consultants told Nick and me that A21 would never work in

Eastern Europe, that it needed much more than a wing and a prayer to fly, we took only part of their advice.

The prayer part.

Now we have offices all over world. A21 works to raise awareness of human trafficking, establish prevention programs in schools and orphanages, represent victims as legal advocates, and give them refuge—in safe houses, then restoration in transition homes.

God didn't remove all the difficulties from our path. Difficulty is part of this world. But God is bigger than any difficulty. He sees above and beyond any obstacle. He leads us a step at a time over the mountains into the valleys he wants us to possess because no prayer is too big for him to answer, no problem too big for him to solve. There is no disease he cannot heal or heart he cannot mend. There is no bondage God cannot break, need he cannot meet, enemy he cannot defeat, or mountain he cannot move.

There is nothing my God cannot do.

I will never forget the day my daughter Catherine came home from children's church with that song, "My God Is So Big," on her lips. As most children do, she kept singing the song over and over as if it were stuck on "repeat" in the CD player: "My God is so big, so strong and so mighty/There's nothing my God cannot do [clap, clap] ..."

Eventually, the endless repetition began to get on my nerves. Maybe it was time to fire the children's pastor—or force her to teach the kids some new songs. I was just about to tell my daughter, "Catie, Mommy needs some quiet time—alone." Then I stopped. *What if this is all Catherine ever knows and believes about God?* I thought. *What if the truth in these simple lyrics is woven into the very fabric of her heart and every fiber of her being? Imagine what could she do, if she truly believed that no difficulty, obstacle, or hurdle could defeat God's plan for her life? Imagine the difficulties she could overcome without a second thought or glance.*

How I wanted that kind of faith.

"My God is so big," I began to sing along with her.

I still face giants, but I'm determined not to be stopped by them.

"Go into all the world," God told me (Matthew 28:19).

He didn't say how. He didn't say if. He just said: Go and look for the lost. Find the missing. Bring them into this land where hope is plentiful. Start where you are, with what you have, however you can.

Throughout this book, I have tried to make the point, in as many ways as I can and as clearly as I can, that God has set before each of us an exciting and world-changing mission. And that he wants to work *in* us, to equip and empower and qualify us, so that he can work *through* us. For some of us, either the mission he calls us to or the prospect of turning our lives over to him so that he can prepare us is daunting. But to live truly *un*daunted, to ask others to have faith, you must summon your own faith in God. You follow a God who is moved by your prayers, and your tears, just as you would be moved by the words and tears of your own child. And when God is moved, you look up and over whatever giant is standing in your way, because God will move him.

After all, God can move mountains. Why would he hesitate to remove a mere giant?

The Challenge

When you decide enough is enough, that the darkness of this world must be lit with the hope of Christ and his transforming love, and that you are a conduit of that love, you will not rest.

Once God opened my eyes to the horrors in this world, my restlessness grew. The horrors were not in another time or place, but next door, along my streets, in my community, and wherever I traveled.

And so many of them could so easily have been mine. My life might not have turned out as it has. I, too, had once been trapped. I, too, had once been unloved, forgotten, and broken. What if I'd remained in that dark place? What if, as number 2508 of 1966, I'd been born in Moldova or Bulgaria or Romania and left in an orphanage instead of a hospital in Sydney, Australia? What if I'd never been adopted by loving, kind, generous parents? What if those who took me home from the hospital were traffickers? What if my abuse had never stopped, if I could not have escaped it?

Every day has been a deeper awakening to this. God has

shaken me alert to the suffering in this world, the imprisonment of people who languish. Sometimes the bars are visible. More often, they're not. What I know for sure is that for all its goodness, all its beauty, this world is too dark for us to be content to slumber. Every dawn is a reminder that we have a new day, another chance to make the difference.

When I lay down to sleep at night, my life seems far removed from the lives of those who are trapped, pleading, broken—worlds apart, in fact. I am happily married, with healthy and happy children, living in a loving and safe home, able to come and go and travel the world with purpose and amazing opportunities to teach and to learn myself. My family and I have food, clothing, shelter, and health care. My future is filled with dreams, plans, goals, vision. I am free. Yet in the work of A21, and in my travels, I meet so many who are languishing, forgotten, without justice, love, hope, or any promise that their lives—or their children's—may someday get better.

Our situations could not be more different—and yet the gap between our lives is, in fact, so very small, so sliver-thin, so . . . cross-shaped.

Standing in that gap is Jesus, who has thrown down his cross as the bridge from the world of darkness into the world of light and freedom, truth and love.

For when we were yet unloved, he loved us.[1]

Before we could be chosen, he chose us.[2]

When we were broken and damaged, feeding on bitterness and blame, he made us whole and showed us how to feast on forgiveness.[3]

When we had no hope, he became our hope.[4]

When we were overbusy with the cares of this world, he interrupted us to show us what is eternal.[5]

When we were lost, he found us, rescued us, and showed us that his mercy and justice will prevail.[6]

When we were disappointed, he sustained us to show us how disappointments can bring us to appointments he ordained.[7]

When we were afraid, he gave us courage, stood with us,

and showed us how to illuminate the darkness with his light.[8]

When things got difficult, he pulled us along and pushed and carried us so that we could pull, push, and carry others.[9]

He owned the cross so that he could make a way across the nightmarish abyss, enabling us to walk through the gap, too, bringing his love and hope and change to a world engulfed by the dark, screaming in fear.

"As you sent me into the world," Jesus prayed, "I have sent them" (John 17:18).

Jesus loves us and chooses us and makes us whole, not only for his pleasure but so that we might join him in reaching a world otherwise lost. He is passionate to save the world and gave his life for that very reason. God "did not send his Son into the world to condemn the world, but to save the world through him" (John 3:17). Jesus commissioned us to go into that same world and to shine his light in the darkness so that others may be rescued and set free.

And yet we slumber. We sleep.

When Jesus said to go into all the world (Matthew 28:19), he didn't mean to wait until morning, or until you get the right job, or find the perfect spouse, or have raised the kids right, or have your house in order, or find a spare weekend. Christ brought us light in the darkness so that we can reach everyone living a nightmare now. He longs to shake us awake so that we can shout out the truth—that humankind is made for eternity but trapped in time, and time is running out. He means for us to be a lantern in the darkness. He means for us to find and rescue others because we know what it is to be lost and then found, hurting and then healed.

He means for us to walk into the gap where he's thrown down the cross, to walk like him, to walk with him.

Unwilling to stay asleep.

Unafraid of the dark.

Unflinching in the face of disappointment.

Unstoppable in the face of difficulty.

Undaunted.

Notes

Chapter 1: The *Schindler's List* Moment

1. Numbers are dehumanizing, desensitizing—and shockingly numbing. For every mass number there are thousands of individuals whose lives are at stake. The UN estimates twenty-seven million people worldwide are slaves, two and half million of whom are trapped in human trafficking. More than eight million children under the age of five die from malnutrition and mostly preventable diseases each year. Almost five thousand people die every day due to HIV/AIDS. More than 884 million people do not have access to safe drinking water sources. At least two thousand children die each day due to poverty. An estimated 121 million people suffer from depression. One million people commit suicide each year. Between 100 and 140 million girls and women live with the consequences of female genital mutilation.

2. Psalm 69:28; 139:16; Isaiah 49:1; Revelation 3:5; 17:8; 20:12–15.

3. Luke 4:18.

Chapter 2: I'm Not Who I Thought I Was

1. Psalm 139:13–16.

2. Romans 8:38–39.

3. John 3:16; 14:1–15.

4. Ephesians 2:10.

5. Deuteronomy 31:6; Psalm 46:1; 63:8; Ephesians 2:1; Hebrews 13:5–6; 1 John 4:8–19.

6. John 8:30–32.

Chapter 3: Number 2508 of 1966

1. Genesis 1:27; Ephesians 2:10.

2. Ephesians 2:10.

3. Deuteronomy 31:6; John 10:27; Hebrews 13:5.

4. Isaiah 49:1 (NKJV).

5. Ibid.

6. Mark 13:31.

7. Isaiah 43:1; Malachi 3:16; Philippians 3:14, 20; 4:3; Revelation 20:15–16.

Chapter 5: Heartbreak — or Breakthrough?

1. "Blessed Be Your Name," by Matt and Beth Redman. Copyright © 2002 Thankyou Music (PRS) (adm. worldwide at EMICMGPublishing.com, excluding Europe which is adm. by Kingswaysongs) All rights reserved. Used by permission.

Chapter 7: I Once Was Lost

1. John 8:12.

Chapter 9: Divine Interruption

1. The family's website is *www.findmadeleine.com*.

Conclusion: The Challenge

1. 1 John 4:19

2. Ephesians 1:4.

3. Colossians 2:13.

4. 1 Peter 1:3.

5. Luke 15.

6. Luke 4:17–21; 1 Peter 2:24.

7. John 6:24–35.

8. John 1 and John 8:12.

9. Matthew 28:18–20; Isaiah 53:4–5.

Acknowledgments

I will be forever grateful to all the people who helped make *Undaunted* a reality. To be honest, I was totally daunted by the prospect of writing this book. It is the one book that I knew I had to write, yet I felt totally inadequate when it came time to put onto paper the words stored in my heart. I now understand as never before that it certainly takes many people to come alongside an author to birth a book. I lack sufficient words to appropriately thank everyone involved in this project both directly and indirectly, but please know that my gratitude flows from the very depths of my being.

I want to thank the entire Zondervan team who became more like family than publishers during this process. If it were not for my executive editor, Sandy Vander Zicht, I am not sure there would even be a book. She believed in me and would not let me give up when I desperately wanted to. Her prayers and those of her Bible study group sustained me throughout this long and, at times, painful process. Special thanks to Greg Clouse for your edits and eye for detail. Tom Dean and team, thank you for helping to get the message out to the broadest possible audience. Robin Phillips, thank you for ensuring that a valuable participant's guide has accompanied the curriculum.

The amazing Jeanette Thomason helped me craft the words that brought the stories to life, and together we processed so much of the struggle of taking what was in my heart and converting it to words. Without her tireless effort and commitment, this book would not be what it is. Liz Heaney was such a gift from God, not only helping to bring out "the book" in the book, but frequently encouraging me and expressing her belief that I could and should write it. I often wonder what would have happened if Dave Lambert did not graciously step in and take the manuscript from where it was to what it has become. I personally think he is a genius.

A number of dear friends walked this journey alongside me and read more revisions of the manuscript than anyone ever should, always offering fresh insights and perspective. A heartfelt thanks goes to Annie Dollarhide, Natalie Laborde, Kristen Morse, and Bianca Olthoff. You will never know how much your love, support, and encouragement helped me to finish this book.

I am so grateful for my senior pastors, Brian and Bobbie Houston, and my Hillsong church family. When I found a "home" in my local church, my journey of restoration and healing truly began. They loved and believed in me when I was young, raw, and very broken. So much of who I am today can be attributed to the local church where I have been planted all of these years.

Because this book contains so much of my own journey, I must also thank my spiritual mother, Joyce Meyer, who believed in me and helped me to press through the pain of my past to lay hold of the promises of God in my future. She is a woman who has exemplified to me in every conceivable way what it is to truly be *undaunted*. She has supported our work in ministry from the beginning and encouraged me as a daughter in the faith always. She is a true hero to me.

Acknowledgments

I could not begin to express my gratitude to Max Lucado for agreeing to write the foreword for this book. His own words have so often been used by God to inspire and encourage me, it is one of the greatest honors of my life that he would so kindly add his strength to my message.

More than anyone else, it is my husband, Nick, and daughters, Catherine and Sophia, who walked through every second of every moment of every hour of every day of every week of every month of every year it has taken me to write *Undaunted*. Only heaven knows the sacrifices they made to allow me to write this book, and I am ever so grateful. My love for them and appreciation of them is indescribable.

I am eternally grateful for and to my Lord and Savior Jesus Christ.

About the Author

Known for her ability to communicate profound messages of hope and inspiration, Christine Caine has a heart for reaching the lost, strengthening leadership, championing the cause of justice, and building the local church globally.

In 2008, Christine and her husband, Nick, founded The A21 Campaign, an organization dedicated to addressing the injustice of human trafficking in the twenty-first Century. A21's comprehensive approach includes raising awareness, preventing future trafficking, taking legal action, and offering support services to survivors.

Christine Caine is an avid believer in the hope-giving power of the local church, and is part of the leadership team at Hillsong Church of Sydney, Australia. She is the author of four books, including *A Life Unleashed* and *The Core Issue*.

THE **A21** CAMPAIGN

99% OF HUMAN TRAFFICKING VICTIMS ARE NOT RESCUED... YET.

When confronted with the horrific statistics surrounding human trafficking, most people are quick to agree on the fact that someone should **do something.** The A21 Campaign was born when we decided to raise our hand and be the ones who would do something. The A21 Campaign was born when we decided to raise our hand and join the ranks of "someone." In 2007, with little knowledge and a lot of passion, we set out to make a difference. Today we are strategically positioned in Europe, North America, and Australia to abolish the injustice of human trafficking and rehabilitate victims.

Today we are strategically positioned in Europe, North America, and Australia to abolish the injustice of human trafficking and rehabilitate its victims.

The goal of A21 is fourfold:

1. Prevent people from being trafficked.

2. Protect those who have been trafficked, and provide support services.

3. Prosecute traffickers, and strengthen legal responses to trafficking.

4. Partner with law enforcement, service providers, and community members to provide a comprehensive front against trafficking.

BECAUSE... everyONE matters.

www.TheA21Campaign.org

Undaunted Study Guide with DVD

Daring to Do What God Calls You to Do

Christine Caine

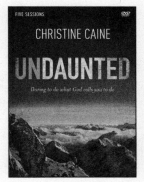

Undaunted by Christine Caine is a compelling five-session video based study with study guide that will take you and your small group on an epic journey through the stages of pain and loss that ultimately lead to hope, healing, and a new beginning. Through Caine's own dramatic life story, you and your small group will be challenged—with God's help—to overcome fear and find your own calling.

Sessions include:

1. The Call
2. Be the Love
3. Be the Hope
4. Be the Change
5. The Challenge

Available in stores and online!